CALIFORNIA REEFS

Happy Birthday,
Leslie,
with much love
Aunt Jeanie
June 1992

CALIFORNIA
REEFS

Chuck Davis

Foreword by Jean-Michel Cousteau

CHRONICLE BOOKS · SAN FRANCISCO

1

Printed in Hong Kong.

Library of Congress Cataloging in Publication Data
Davis, Chuck, 1954–
    California reefs / Chuck Davis ; foreword by
Jean-Michel Cousteau.
        p.   cm.
    ISBN 0-8118-0072-5. —ISBN 0-87701-787-5 (pbk.)
    1. Reef biology—California.   2. Reef biology—
California—Pictorial works.   I. Title.
QH105.C2D38   1991
574.9′1794—dc20   91-8810
                                          CIP

Editing: Deborah Stone and Mary Anne Stewart
Book and cover design: Robin Weiss Graphic Design
Composition: Ann Flanagan Typography, Berkeley

PLATE 1. *Norris' top snail, San Clemente Island.*

PLATE 2. *Giant kelp forest with garibaldi,
Santa Catalina Island.*

PLATE 3. *Club anemones, Stillwater Cove,
Monterey.*

Distributed in Canada by Raincoast Books,
112 East Third Avenue, Vancouver, B.C. V5T 1C8

10 9 8 7 6 5 4 3 2 1

Chronicle Books
275 Fifth Street
San Francisco, CA 94103

TABLE OF CONTENTS

To Norma

*Without her undying patience,
understanding, and encouragement,
this book would never
have come to be.*

3

ACKNOWLEDGMENTS

Throughout the production of this book, many people have given generously of their time and expertise. I would like to extend a very special thank-you to Jean-Michel Cousteau, who kindly wrote a foreword for me, and to Dr. Wheeler J. North, who undertook a major review of my text and provided painstaking notes to assure its scientific accuracy. I would also like to thank Dr. Richard C. Murphy, Dr. Robert Norris, Dr. Mia Tegner, and Dr. Richard Zimmerman for their scientific help and advice, and David Barich, Lisa Howard, and the staff of Chronicle Books for their enthusiasm for this book when it was still a concept and for their help in steering it to final publication.

Over the years I have been blessed with a small army of friends who have also helped immeasurably. Many have assisted me on and under the sea; others have generously shared their knowledge of underwater photography, writing, publishing, marine science, diving, dive sites, and equipment. To all of them I would like to extend a heartfelt thanks:

Aqua Vision Systems, Inc.; Alan Broder/A B Sea Photo; Ernest H. Brooks II and the Brooks Institute; Jim Carr; Captain Jon Capella and the crew of the dive boat *Xeno;* the Cabrillo Marine Museum; Captain Jacques-Yves Cousteau and the Cousteau Society; Bob Cranston; Michel Deloire; Scott Frier; Rusty Geller; Dan Gross; Ann Guilfoyle; Stuart Hall; Hillary Hauser; Peter Howorth; Al and Laury Huelga and the Aquarius Dive Shops; Captains Jim Ingram/Ken Kivett and the crew of the dive boat *Westerly;* Joseph Leonardo, the late Frank Leonardo, and Leonardo and Son Skin Diver's Supply; Marina Dive and Sport; Oceanic USA; Eddie Paul; Louis Prezelin; Ron Robinson; Sonic Research, Inc.; Peter Romano; Bob Talbot; U.S. Divers Company; and Mal Wolfe.

Finally, to my late father, my mother, my stepfather, my brother, Mark, and sister, Kathy, thanks for all the years of warm understanding and encouragement. Your love helped foster this book.

FOREWORD

When Chuck Davis takes us as readers from our familiar terrestrial world into the undersea majesty of the California reefs, we are blessed with a rare and percipient guide. Chuck is not only a very talented photographer, but an explorer with a wide scientific background, a sense of observation, and a beguiling touch of humor. He is also adept at horizontal thinking, which allows him to make connections and identify relationships that do not appear obvious at first.

Through Chuck Davis's photographs we swim in a world of breathtaking but fragile beauty. Through his eyes we discover the connections of this liquid realm where everything is a necessary, inseparable part of a giant living puzzle—a puzzle upon which humans put enormous pressure. May this book help us to acquire a little more knowledge and much inspiration with which to protect what we have come to love.

Jean-Michel Cousteau

PLATE 4. *Jack mackerel, Santa Catalina Island.*

INTRODUCTION

Even if you're not a diver but live in California or have visited there, chances are you've driven close to one of the state's many submerged reefs. As near as a few hundred yards from certain sections of California's routes 1, 101, and 405, where the roadbed swerves close to the sea, an extensive marine ecosystem lies hidden beneath a blanket of emerald-green waters.

Here, myriad species of fish, invertebrates, marine mammals, and algae participate in a saga of life and death—and survival—in vast undersea communities that lie, for the most part, silent and unseen.

Usually evidenced by a telltale floating kelp mat, these living conglomerations of biology and bedrock extend intermittently along much of California's eleven-hundred-mile coastline. Southward, reefs dominated by forests of the giant kelp plant *Macrocystis pyrifera* reach beyond the Mexican border into Baja California; to the north, they extend well into central California and also embrace the state's many offshore islands. Although reefs dominated by giant kelp are not as prevalent in northern California, reef communities with other dominant brown algae thrive all the way to the Oregon border and beyond.

In the colloquial sense and by formal definition, the word *reef* is a vague and confusing term. Dictionaries usually define it as an area of sand, rock, or coral that rises to or near the surface of a body of water. This is undoubtedly a practical definition for mariners, but it falls short for divers and fishermen, all of whom know that there are deep reefs, shallow reefs, and even, in some cases, artificial reefs where all manner of debris,

PLATE 5. *Reef ledge with club anemones and orange hydrocoral, Cypress Point, Carmel.*

PLATE 6. *Blackeye goby with mussel shells and orange sea cucumbers, Santa Cruz Island.*

6

from old automobile tires to concrete blocks and retired trolley cars, have been placed on the ocean bottom to attract fish. For the sake of clarity, this book
features only naturally occurring reefs off the coast of
California and its outlying islands.

The sea floor bordering California, much like the
coast itself, is comprised of a series of mountainous
ridges, deep canyons, and flat plains. Dramatic earth
movements and prehistoric ice ages, which affected
the volume of the world's oceans, have greatly influ-
enced the topography and character of California's
reefs.

Mean sea level along the coast of California has not
remained constant in the recent geological past; over
thousands of years it has risen and dropped several
hundred feet. Bedrock submerged four hundred feet
off southern California, for example, has been scarfed
and wave-cut by surf that pounded against these former shorelines thirty thousand years ago. It is believed
that the sea level along California advanced and receded dramatically over many millennia. Approximately seven thousand years ago, the Pacific rested
about one hundred feet below our present shoreline.
It has risen steadily ever since. Today, divers swim in
one hundred feet of water over reef ledges that were
once ancient shorelines: shorelines that endured the
same landshaping forces of sun, wind, rain, runoff,
and oceanic water movements that today's coastline
experiences. Now buried by a blanket of sea water,
weathered boulders with deep cracks and crevices,
wave-cut ledges with steep cliffs, and canyons cut by
ancient river beds now shelter and are sheltered by
marine life.

The very same mountain-building processes and

PLATE 7. *Reef ledge detail with leather star and orange
hydrocoral, Inner Carmel Pinnacle, Carmel.*

land slippages that have made California famous for its earthquakes have also, over the past thirty million years or so, contributed to the state's underwater geologic formations.

At some parts of the California coast—Gaviota, for example—the bedrock both above and below water is folded and bent as a result of local earth movements. These tilted rocks have been weathered and eroded,

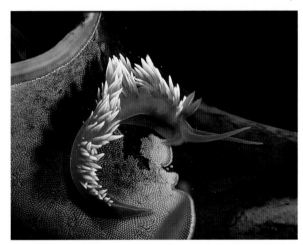

8

creating an excellent reef substrate. Divers can examine this phenomenon at nearby Refugio State Park, where the sea bed drops off gradually with a series of tilted ledges that extends several hundred yards offshore.

At other offshore locations, such as the Farallon Islands near San Francisco, the Channel Islands near Santa Barbara, and Santa Catalina Island off the coast of Los Angeles, the tips of undersea mountains protrude above the ocean's surface, forming isolated marine ecosystems. Initially formed between five to fifteen million years ago when blocks of the earth's crust were faulted and uplifted, these areas have since partially sunk back into the sea as the sea bed subsided and the global sea level rose. Today the submerged

parts of these islands, which at one time were parts of above-water mountain chains, support some of California's most pristine and awe-inspiring undersea areas. At a number of locations, such as the east end of San Clemente Island and the northwest coast of Santa Catalina Island, the reefs are characterized by dramatic steeply sloping walls of volcanic bedrock that plummet into deep water. As varied as California's rugged coastline is, so too are the frameworks of its submerged reefs.

Differences in sea bed topography and prevailing oceanic conditions no doubt cause some variation in

PLATE 8. *Spanish shawl nudibranch on elkhorn kelp with encrusting bryozoans, Santa Catalina Island.*

PLATE 9. *Giant kelpfish, Santa Catalina Island.*

9

species from reef to reef in California. Changes in water temperature may cause the same species to be found at different depths along different parts of the coast. Red abalone, for example, can be found in shallow water in northern California but are usually seen in deep water in southern California. While the depths that animals live at can vary, they prefer similar temperatures; shallow-water temperatures in the north where ocean water is cooler may be the same as deep-water temperatures in the south. In other cases, certain marine creatures have a distinct preference for northern or southern habitats. The garibaldi fish, for example, is prevalent in southern California waters but rare north of Point Conception. The rock greenling, on the other hand, is rare south of Point Concep-

tion but more common in the cooler waters of central and northern California. The photographs in this collection, even though taken from a number of different locations, depict marine life that with few exceptions can be found on reefs throughout the state.

There are good days and bad days underwater off the coast of California. At worst, a violent winter storm surge can whip up chilly waters, churning sand and bottom sediment and creating near-zero underwater visibility. Such conditions make diving difficult and underwater photography nearly impossible. At the

---

PLATE 10. *Octopus silhouette, Santa Rosa Island.*

PLATE 11. *Yellow zooanthid anemones on gorgonian, Santa Catalina Island.*

other extreme are many consecutive days of glassy calm seas in the late summer and fall, with underwater visibility of about one hundred feet. On many more days, conditions fall somewhere in between. The undersea world off California is not always a tranquil place, but it is always a fascinating place.

It is understandable, yet still regrettable, that most people's perception of the riches harbored by California's coastal reefs stops at the ocean interface where sunlight and wind create golden flickers in the floating brown canopy. *California Reefs* seeks to expand that perception.

The pages that follow will take you on a journey to an undersea world, a world of contrasts: of color and darkness, warmth and cold, and even tragedy and comedy; a world so different from what we perceive as our own that it at first seems to defy comprehension. Yet, remarkably, it is very much a part of us.

While this book's title might suggest a treatise on the many different reefs bordering coastal California, it in fact treats the California reef as a single entity, one single living superorganism that is connected to all other life forms in California and the planet.

As you swim over a reef ledge on a calm, clear day, towering stalks of giant kelp converge toward the surface, where tightly focused rays of sunlight flicker through the thick surface canopy, making shimmering silhouettes of schools of fish. A bat ray swims past, eaglelike, or a friendly pod of sea lions descends upon you, seemingly out of nowhere. There is magic here; it is not just a synergy between algae, fish, and invertebrates. Like the sequoia forest it so closely resembles, the sea forest and the reef it shadows has a spiritual power that can't be quantified: it is the power that motivates inward reflection, creates emotions, and inspires visions.

12

The images presented here were photographed over a twelve-year period while I explored a variety of reefs at Point Lobos and the Monterey Peninsula; Santa Barbara; the Santa Barbara Channel; the nearby Channel Islands of Anacapa, Santa Cruz, Santa Rosa, and San Miguel. Further south I explored reefs at Leo Carrillo State Park near Malibu; San Diego's La Jolla area; and the islands of Santa Catalina, San Clemente, San Nicolas, Santa Barbara, and Cortez Banks.

After underwater explorations of more than a decade, I realize how much there is still to explore. To include photographs of all the species of marine life in California waters is far beyond the scope of this book. What is presented here, though, is a collection of some of the state's most prevalent undersea life.

By design, this book contains not only images that depict the familiar three-dimensional world but also those that are more abstract. The initial view of the undersea world, more often than not, tends to accentuate the great differences between terrestrial and aquatic existence, while a closer view isolates and intensifies the contrasts of pure colors, textures, and designs—images that, if taken out of context, might not be perceived as belonging to the world of fish and invertebrates, or even the ocean. They are life patterns, composed of cells and living protoplasm, just as we are.

I hope that you, too, will enjoy, as I have so many times, discovering a little bit of yourselves within *California Reefs*.

Chuck Davis

PLATE 12. *Surfgrass detail, Santa Barbara Island.*

PLATE 13. *Red gorgonian detail, Santa Cruz Island.*

PLATE 14. *California sea hare skin pattern, Anacapa Island.*

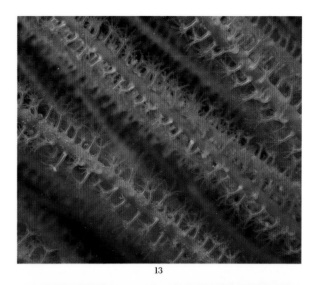

13

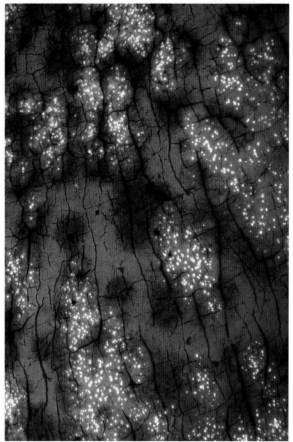

14

UNDERSEA
FORESTS

Like most things occurring in nature, there is no blueprint for a California reef. In some areas off the state's coast, the beach and ocean bottom are rocky and the sea bed plummets quickly into deep water while a floating giant kelp mat forms a narrow belt close to shore. At other locations, the shore is sandy and the sea bed deepens gradually; the sandy near-shore bottom may be scattered with areas of exposed bedrock perhaps one hundred yards or more from shore. At some locations west of Santa Barbara, belts of sand run parallel to shore, alternating with exposed bands of bedrock. Here, the height of exposed ledges and the depth of the water increase gradually for several hundred yards off the beach. Other locations along the California coast may combine many of these characteristics, for there are no absolutes in nature.

A great deal about a reef's topography can be detected from above water by studying the floating kelp mat and how the waves break over the area. Generally giant kelp (and some twenty other species of kelp that grow in California waters) only attach to hard surfaces. Thus, if kelp is present, chances are excellent there is a rocky substrate. The surf offers different clues to bottom topography: Waves that break suddenly and close to shore indicate a steeply sloping ocean bottom. Conversely, waves gradually forming over one hundred yards or more before breaking onshore suggest a gradually sloping sea bed. In places where ledges or rock pinnacles rise close to the ocean's surface some distance from the beach, waves may break far offshore, indicating a reef, and then re-form before breaking again onshore.

PLATE 15. *Blacksmith school in giant kelp forest, Santa Barbara Island.*

PLATE 16. *Giant kelp, apical tip detail, Santa Catalina Island.*

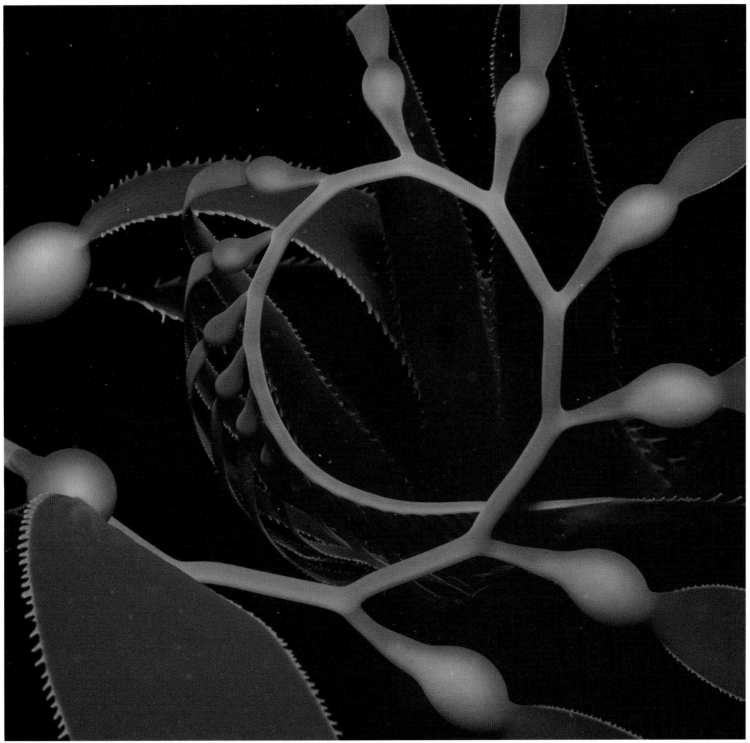

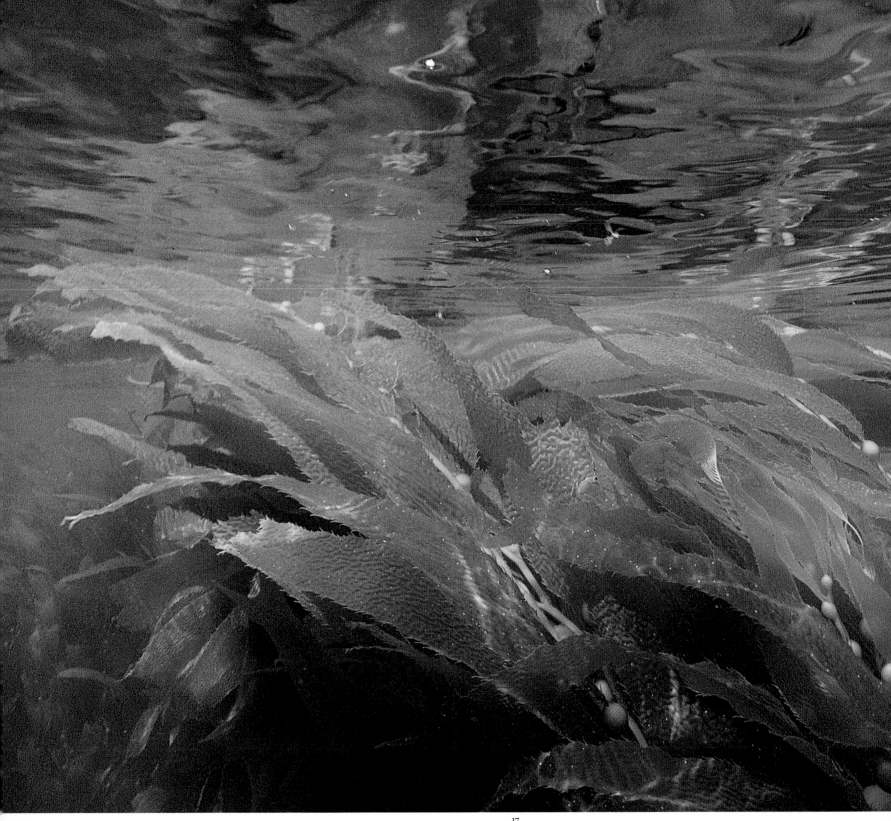

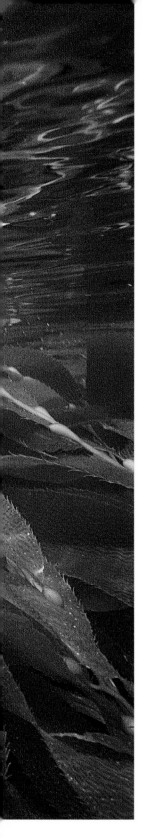

18

While California reefs occur in a variety of shapes and sizes, they share many common denominators. In terms of sheer biomass and its contribution to other marine life as a source of refuge and food, the giant kelp plant *Macrocystis pyrifera* is undoubtedly the most dominant life form on all reefs from central California to Baja California, in Mexico. Flourishing mostly in cool waters off the Pacific coasts of the United States, Canada, and south to Mexico's Baja Peninsula, giant kelp is the world's fastest-growing marine plant. Under ideal conditions it is capable of up to two feet of growth per day. Varieties of *Macrocystis* are also found in widely scattered areas of the Southern Hemisphere, such as the eastern coast of Tasmania and areas of New Zealand, Argentina, Chile, and South Africa.

Giant kelp grows best when sea-water temperatures remain below 70°F. Because of this, *Macrocystis* doesn't occur off coasts bathed by tropical waters. In some cases, however, it can tolerate periods of warm temperatures. Kelp plants in Baja California, for example, can withstand elevated summer temperatures by adjusting to changes in their environment. In contrast to these southern kelp plants, *Macrocystis* forests farther north on the California coast cannot make this adjustment; the consequences of prolonged warm temperatures can be devastating to them.

Biologists believe that the direct link between kelp survival and ocean temperature is a tenuous one: sea water nutrients are believed to be of more critical importance. While it is true that giant kelp favors coasts with cool waters, these waters owe their cool-

PLATE 17. *Side view of giant kelp canopy taken from just beneath the ocean surface, Santa Barbara Island.*

PLATE 18. *Giant kelp haptera detail, Santa Catalina Island.*

19

ness in part to upwelling of the deep ocean that delivers vital nutrients to surface waters. It may very well be that giant kelp plants in Baja California can withstand extended periods of warm weather simply because there is just enough local upwelling taking place to periodically pulse enough nutrients upward to sustain them.

For reasons still not understood by scientists, approximately every two to ten years, our planet experiences a dramatic shift in its prevailing weather patterns, which markedly affects normal climatic conditions in many parts of the world. This global condition, known as El Niño, affects California's normal wind and temperature patterns; water temperatures may be elevated from 4°F to 10°F or more, and weather conditions can range from severe drought to violent storms followed by floods. In Spanish, El Niño literally means "the child." The name refers to the birth of Christ; in South America the drastic elevation in water temperature that occurs during El Niño is often experienced in December. El Niño is believed to originate when changes in weather patterns in the tropical Pacific alter the normal flow of equatorial ocean currents and surface trade winds. Because of these temporary changes, more warm ocean water flows to the western coast of South America and then northward along the California coast.

Elevated water temperatures and reduction of nutrients during the most recent El Niño, in 1982–1983, resulted in the devastation of many miles of California's giant kelp forests. It was nearly two years before these formerly healthy stands began to recover.

Normally, though, the California coast offers an ideal environment for kelp growth. Not only is the entire coast bathed by chilly waters from the California Current, which moves water south from the Gulf of Alaska, but regional winds also create an upwelling from the deep ocean that contributes added nutrients and accelerates kelp growth.

Upwelling occurs when winds push surface water away from the coast (to a lesser degree, local currents can also contribute to upwelling). The world's major ocean currents form large circular orbits, or gyres, which flow clockwise in the Northern Hemisphere and counter-clockwise in the Southern Hemisphere. Because of the earth's Coriolis effect, these currents experience a slight right-hand deflection of their energy and surface waters in the Northern Hemisphere; in the Southern Hemisphere, this same phenomenon occurs, but with a left-hand deflection of energy and surface water. Because prevailing winds along the California coast are from the north and west, the south sides of peninsulas, the north sides of bays, and the parts of the coast that are oriented east to west tend to experience the most upwelling.

When surface waters are pushed offshore, ocean up-

PLATE 19. *Swell shark egg casing attached to haptera of giant kelp holdfast, Santa Catalina Island.*

PLATE 20. *Giant kelp forest with holdfast in foreground, Santa Barbara Island.*

PLATE 21 NEXT PAGE. *Giant kelpfish detail, Santa Catalina Island.*

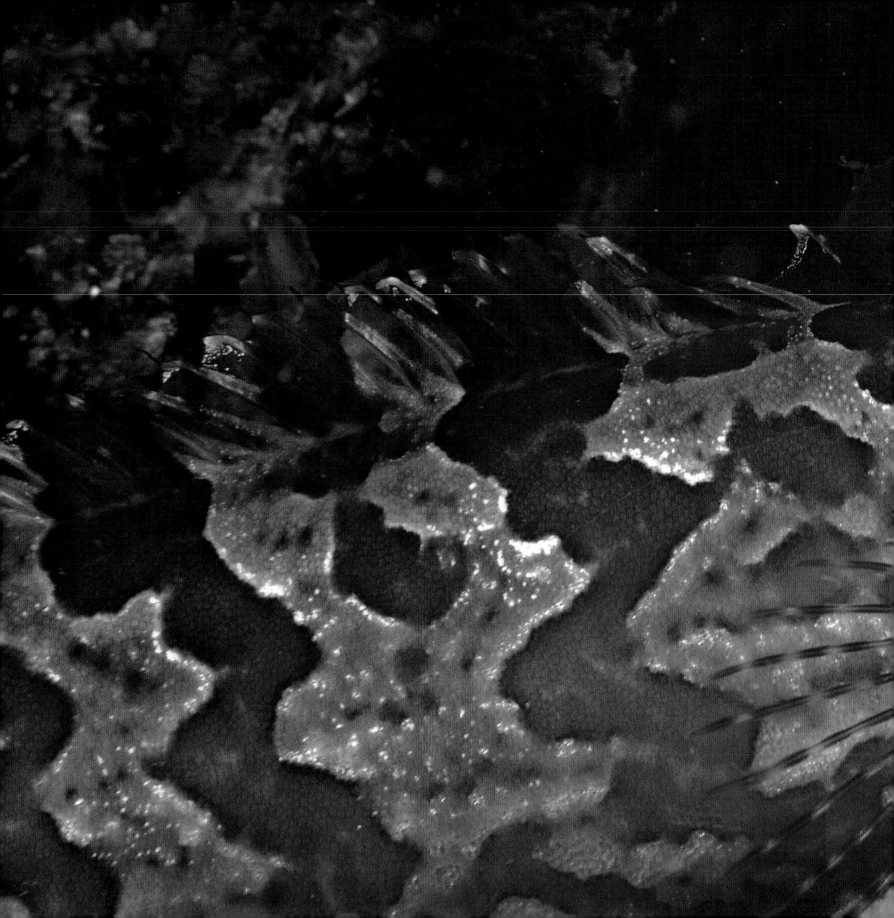

welling occurs as warmer surface waters are replaced by deeper colder waters that rise up from the ocean bottom. Upwelled waters are rich with nutrients and minerals resulting from organic matter that has fallen to the deep ocean. Deeper, colder bottom waters, relatively devoid of light and life, are a nutrient bank for the shallower coastal ocean. Loans from the depths are repaid when upwelled nutrients are converted to plants and then animals. Biological wastes and eventually death result in nutrients completing the cycle as organic matter drifts back down again to begin the process anew.

Although the California Current flows slowly and steadily down the entire West Coast, it has a greater influence on northern and central California, where it meanders in close to the continent during late summer and fall. South of Point Conception, where the coast cuts in eastward at the great California Bight, the California Current remains farther offshore.

In contrast to the south-flowing California Current, a less prevalent current called the Davidson Current flows intermittently from south to north off the coast. Although it normally bypasses southern California, it comes close to the central and northern coast during winter, warming the normally chilly waters there.

Waters in southern California south of Point Conception have warmer year-round temperatures than central and northern California due to solar heating and less mixing of the ocean within the California Bight. As a result, there exists a slight variation in

---

PLATE 22. *Giant kelp detail showing stipe, pneumatocysts, blades, and bryozoan encrustations, Santa Catalina Island.*

PLATE 23. *Anthopleura anemone on haptera of giant kelp holdfast, Santa Barbara Island.*

PLATE 24. *Giant kelpfish nestled in giant kelp fronds, Santa Catalina Island.*

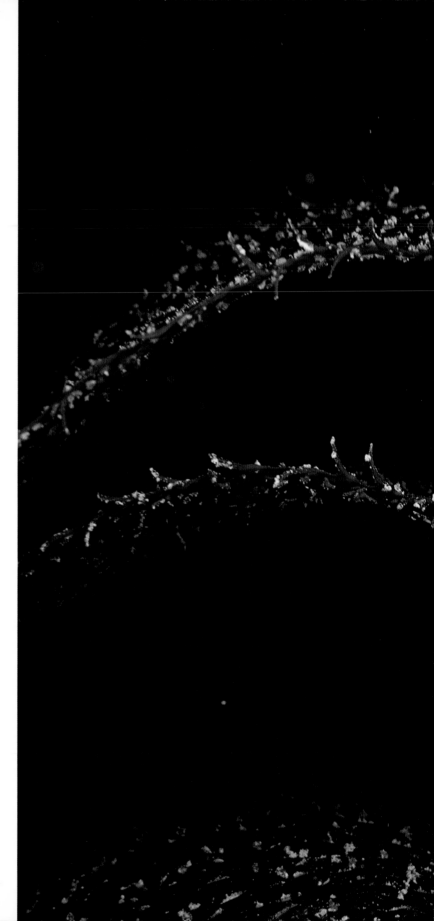

23

24

22

25

26

species from north to south.

From the surface, giant kelp may seem a nuisance rather than an aesthetic life form and valuable resource. It fouls boat propellers, snags fishing lines, obstructs swimming, and attracts beach flies when it washes ashore, a dying, twisted rubbery mess. In its living state, however, it appears much different from the lifeless mass strewn on beaches.

Kelp grows underwater in easily navigated vertical columns that resemble the tree trunks of terrestrial forests. But a kelp forest is dramatically different. Unlike terrestrial plants that transport nourishment upward from root systems, the giant kelp plant doesn't have roots in the truest sense of the word. It must use its entire surface area to absorb nutrients from sea water. It also relies heavily on its surface canopy to capture solar energy. The products of photosynthesis are then conducted downward to low-light areas in a process called translocation. By this means, the plant forms extensive undersea forests that thrive in the shadow of its surface umbrella.

Instead of roots, giant kelp has a rootlike anchor called a *holdfast*. The holdfast is comprised of a conical pile of pencil-sized rubbery strands called *haptera*. The haptera exert a tenacious grip on the ocean bottom and prevent the plant from drifting away.

The holdfast gives rise to bundles of strands called *stipes* that may reach two-hundred-foot lengths. The stipes are buoyed by small bladders filled with gas (nitrogen, carbon dioxide, and carbon monoxide) called *pneumatocysts*. Leaves or *blades* grow from the stipes and, collectively, each stipe with all of its bladders and blades is termed a *frond*.

Even though individual kelp fronds continually sprout and die off, the holdfast itself lives on. Holdfasts have been known to last ten years or more and reach eight- to ten-foot diameters. As the plant grows, new haptera spread out over the old so that a cross-section of an older holdfast will reveal a dark brown central area composed of the oldest, dead haptera; a middle area of more fibrous, but still functional haptera; and an outer layer of the youngest and most actively growing ones.

Though a wide variety of plants and animals inhabit California coastal waters, giant kelp forms the spinal column of the reef. A single *Macrocystis* plant has been known to harbor more than five hundred thousand individual sea creatures, many of them microscopic in size; the kelp forest as a whole offers food and refuge to an estimated eight hundred species of animals and some one hundred thirty species of plants.

Biologists believe that in the absence of giant kelp most or all of these species would probably adapt and survive, in small numbers, near or within the reef's confines. Even though resident animals could probably endure without it, the kelp offers an enhanced environment with more places to hide and more food to eat. The kelp also provides the reef with a physical barrier against storms, buffering it against heavy waves and violent bottom surge.

Submerged within a kelp forest reef are distinct zones of life. In the midwater area from just beneath the canopy, downward to near the top of the reef ledge, schools of fish may abound. Blue rockfish, mackerel, perch, and even, at times, barracuda are just a few of the species that sweep through the open areas of the kelp forest, their schools expanding and

PLATE 25. *California sea lions, Santa Barbara Island.*

PLATE 26. *Giant kelpfish near holdfast of giant kelp; individual on right is gravid female about to lay eggs, Santa Catalina Island.*

contracting as they make their way among the kelp stalks in search of food—or in an effort not to become food. A school of blacksmith, the most commonly seen fish in southern California, retreats into the protection of the kelp stalks as a diver approaches; soon, though, the school slowly emerges, the bluish-gray bodies of the fish suspended almost motionless as hungry mouths nip at current-borne plankton. By day blacksmiths feed in midwater aggregations on the up-current sides of kelp forests; at dusk they retreat below into the protection of shelter holes and crevices. By feeding in daylight and defecating at night in their shelter holes, the blacksmiths transport and recycle nutrients throughout the kelp forest, their feces becoming food for bottom-dwelling reef creatures.

In this midwater zone, a menagerie of creatures can also be found on the kelp itself. A large purplish sea hare grazes across a kelp blade; a member of the Mollusk phylum, the sea hare is closely related to the snail, although through evolution the sea hare has lost its shell. Nearby, a close relative of the sea hare, a Norris' top snail with its fiery red mantle, slithers across a kelp stipe licking the cells and other micro-algae on the stipe's surface. Kelp snails, like sea hares, have a rasplike tongue called a *radula*, which they use to lick surface algae off rocks and off other larger algae.

A number of different species of fish can be found

PLATE 27. *Norris' top snail with calcareous coralline algae and barnacle encrusting its shell, Santa Cruz Island.*

PLATE 28. *Carinated dove snail on giant kelp pneumato-cysts, Ledbetter's Point, Santa Barbara.*

PLATE 29. *Norris' top snail on giant kelp stipe, San Clemente Island.*

PLATE 30. *Purple-ringed top snail on giant kelp, Monterey.*

PLATE 31. *California sea hare on giant kelp blade, Santa Barbara Island.*

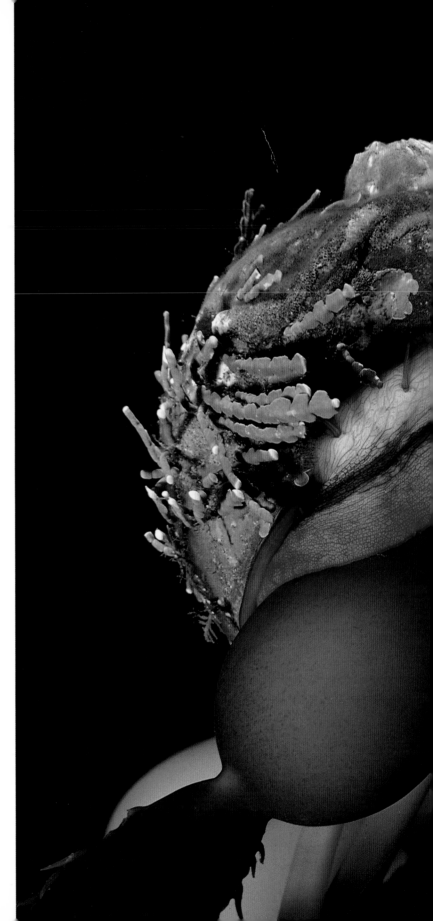

27

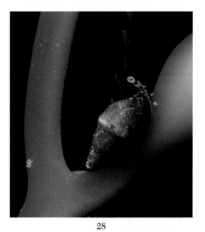

28

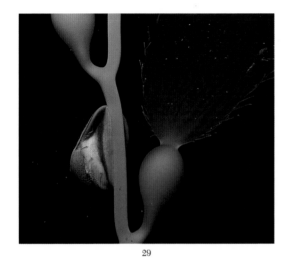

29

30

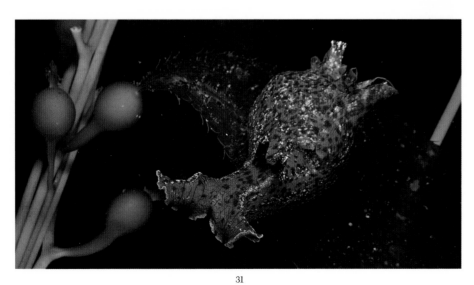

31

hiding within the kelp blades or perched in the leathery kelp stipes. Rockfish sometimes wedge themselves between the stipes; other fish, such as the giant kelpfish, lie among the blades and mimic the kelp's coloration. They look remarkably like a blade of kelp but are more easily seen when they swim between the kelp stalks in search of their diet of small fish, shrimp, and tiny crustaceans.

Closer examination of a kelp stalk may reveal that clean, new stalks rise buoyantly next to aging weathered ones. The older blades hang heavily on the stalk, their surfaces encrusted with tiny invertebrates called bryozoans. Some of these are fuzzy and brownish-red, others are pure white and form a crusty covering resembling frosting. Though a burden to the kelp, bryozoans provide a source of food for reef fish such as señoritas, which specialize in nipping off these encrustations with their sharp teeth.

Usually, the oldest kelp blades will be riddled with holes after being chewed upon by hungry reef crea-

tures. Older kelp fronds and their blades die off by a phenomenon called sloughing, which benefits both the kelp plant and other reef creatures. When older blades fall away, they make way for new, more buoyant ones that will be much more efficient at gathering sunlight and aiding photosynthesis. If the fronds lived longer, they would become so heavy with encrustations that the whole plant might sink. Another benefit of sloughing is that it provides a large food source for algae-consuming fish and invertebrates that eat the kelp as it drifts through the kelp forest down to the reef floor.

The giant kelp plant has a short life span by human standards. The dying kelp blades are remarkably

PLATE 32. *Aging giant kelp blades with eroded surface and encrusting bryozoans.*

PLATE 33. *Giant kelp blade detail with bryozoan colonies, San Clemente Island.*

PLATE 34. *Aging giant kelp blades, with bryozoans, Santa Catalina Island.*

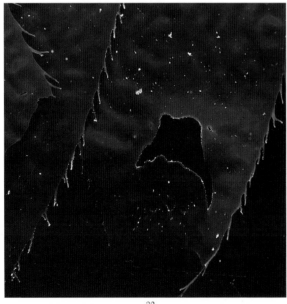

32

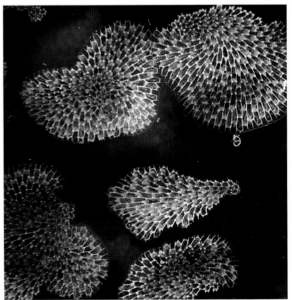

33

35

36

young—perhaps five to six months old. During its life-time, though, the kelp grows prodigiously and repro-duces constantly by vegetative and by sexual means.

In sexual reproduction, spores are dispersed by special blades near the holdfast called *sporophylls*. The sporophylls release microscopic *zoospores* into the ocean; the zoospores settle and later develop into what are called male and female *gametophytes*. These in turn produce eggs and sperm and, upon fertiliza-tion, an embryonic plant with a single heart-shaped blade called a *sporophyte*. In time, if it finds sufficient light and space on the kelp forest floor and if it can survive algae-grazing predators such as sea urchins and abalone, the tiny sporophyte will grow in length as its single blade undergoes numerous microscopic cell divisions. Within eight to nine months, depending upon conditions, the sporophyte grows into an adult giant kelp with fronds stretching to the ocean's sur-face. Its reproductive blades will be capable of pro-ducing spores and sporophytes of its own.

Many environmental factors control kelp growth, but light and sea-water temperature are probably two of the most important. In clear waters, giant kelp has been known to grow in depths of up to one hundred thirty feet, but because of water turbidity and the subsequent loss of light, it more commonly inhabits depths from twenty to eighty feet.

Even though a mature kelp frond begins to wither away or slough after only four or five months, the kelp

PLATE 35. *Blood star with giant kelp holdfast, San Clemente Island.*

PLATE 36. *California spiny lobster on giant kelp stalk, San Nicolas Island.*

PLATE 37. *Giant kelp forest with garibaldi, Santa Catalina Island.*

forest as a whole survives and can regenerate several times each year. It may take a decade or so, but like all living things, the holdfast will finally die, usually the victim of predators or winter storms. Predators like the spiny sea urchin or tiny bug-like crustaceans called kelp gribbles can slowly do enough physical damage to the haptera to cause the holdfast to lose its grip. (Kelp gribbles chew into and tunnel throughout the interior of the haptera; urchins, on the other hand, consume the outer haptera.)

In the early 1960s, urchin predation became so rampant in southern California that kelp forests in San Diego's Point Loma and Los Angeles's Palos Verdes Peninsula nearly disappeared. Studies of the area headed by Dr. Wheeler J. North and sponsored by the University of California's Institute of Marine Resources in San Diego, the California Department of Fish and Game, and the Water Pollution Control Board led to some interesting discoveries. Biologists found that human removal of a prime urchin consumer, the sea otter, coupled with increased coastal sewage dumping, which urchins thrive in, may have knocked the kelp forest ecosystem out of balance.

Hunted nearly to extinction by fur trappers during the 1800s and early 1900s, the California sea otter, *Enhydra lutris*, remains on the endangered species list. It inhabits state waters from the Santa Cruz area southward to San Luis Obispo. Biologists consider sea otters to be some of the youngest of marine mammals, more closely related to their cousins the weasels than to other marine mammals such as seals or sea lions. Although they have a thick coat of fur, otters have no insulating blubber to protect them from the effects of heat loss in cool sea water; consequently, they must eat voraciously, feeding night and day to fuel their metabolism. Otters have excellent dexterity with their front paws; they can often be seen lying in the kelp canopy, sometimes wrapped in a thick ball of kelp fronds, using a rock or other tool to break open clams or urchins. Abalone, crabs, sea stars, and kelp snails are also on the otters' diet.

During the 1950s and early 1960s, minimally treated sewage was dumped close to shore directly into San Diego Bay, where it dispersed out over the adjacent coastline and kelp forests. Biologists believe that the sewage, with its high levels of suspended solid materials, was a key factor in the demise of local kelp forests. As the solids settled out of the water column, they formed sediment on the reefs that prevented the formation of young kelp plants. Suspended materials created an additional problem by clouding the water and reducing the amount of light available for photosynthesis. In 1962 the sewage outfall was extended almost three miles offshore and dispersed in two hundred feet of water; primary treatment of the

---

PLATE 38. *California sea lion in giant kelp forest, Santa Barbara Island.*

PLATE 39. *California sea otter, Lovers' Cove, Monterey.*

effluent was also initiated at this time. With these improvements, local kelp forests made an almost immediate recovery. The recovery was so dramatic that some researchers believe there is a direct correlation between reducing the amount of solids in sewage and extending kelp boundaries.

The urchin infestation that decimated southern California reefs during this time may very well have just been a symptom of a reef system highly stressed by municipal wastes. Whether the urchin plague was the direct result of the otters' removal or whether the calamity was the result of many factors is uncertain. Researchers still debate whether this type of kelp forest devastation is part of a natural cycle or if human intervention is the cause.

Urchins are not necessarily the archenemies of kelp holdfasts; generally they feed on the dead or dying kelp fronds that litter the reef floor. Only when insufficient supplies of kelpshed exist do they turn their appetites toward living kelp plants.

Nevertheless, a successful eradication program, sponsored largely by a private kelp harvesting company, eventually reduced the urchin population, and the kelp forests returned. Since then, a successful red urchin fishery has developed in California, possibly helping to keep urchin populations in check. (After the urchins are shucked and cleaned in processing plants on shore, most of them are shipped to Japan and consumed as a sushi delicacy called *uni*.)

Over time, violent winter storms, not urchins, probably take the heaviest toll on kelp. Powerful waves and the accompanying bottom surge rip the holdfasts from the sea bed. After a giant kelp plant has been

PLATE 40. *Harbor seal in giant kelp forest, off Cannery Row, Monterey.*

torn from the reef, it may wreak further damage as it drifts through the kelp forest, entangling and tearing away at other healthy plants. While drifting kelp plants or kelp paddies have been known to float out to sea and continue growing for a time, eventually becoming a reef unto themselves, much if not most of the uprooted kelp will wash to shore as kelpwrack.

As a marine ecosystem, the sea forest harbors an immeasurable and somewhat intangible wealth. It was estimated in the early 1970s that every square mile of kelp reef off the coast of California represents approximately one million dollars annually to local economies, largely contributed by commercial harvesting. Special ships use rotating blades similar to a giant hedge trimmer to snip the kelp off just below the ocean's surface; the kelp is then hauled aboard with conveyors. Cutting does little or no harm to the kelp forest; some researchers believe it stimulates new growth. The kelp is processed onshore, and a colloidal substance called algin is extracted. Algin (a commercial name) is an excellent emulsifying and thickening agent that makes it possible to combine water with oily liquids. Algin has more than one hundred commercial applications in the manufacture of such things as ice cream, cosmetics, paints, pharmaceuticals, animal food, latex rubber, and even welding rods. In recent years, kelp has also been used experimentally in methane gas production and is seen by some researchers as a possible alternative energy source for the twenty-first century. Test production so far, how-

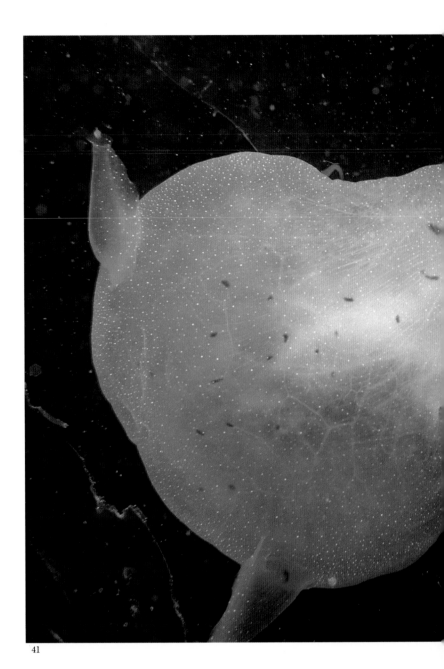

41

PLATE 41. *Lion nudibranch on giant kelp blade, Monterey.*

PLATE 42. *Nudibranch egg ribbon and giant kelp blade, Santa Rosa Island.*

PLATE 43. *Northern kelp crab on giant kelp blade, Monterey.*

42

43

ever, has fallen short of expectations and economic yields.

The tangible assets of a giant kelp forest, which also include commercial and sport fishing, boating, and diving, no doubt add up to an impressive figure for the economist. For the artist and naturalist, however, the intangibles represent even greater riches, riches that all the world's dollars could not buy.

As often happens when I dive in a kelp forest, so much life abounds that I'm sometimes confused about where to point my camera. It is the kelp itself that wins out time and again. For countless chilly hours I have peered through my camera's viewfinder watching geometric shapes and line patterns appear and disappear before my eyes. A section of kelp frond, framed vertically, with its symmetrical sequence of spherical floats, resembles a delicate golden lacework in one instant; in another, it recoils with the pull of the waves into a pinwheel, its blades trailing off in a spiral. The kelp is priceless, a living, pliable sculpture, always moving, always changing with the pull of the tides and the pulsing of waves.

PLATE 44. *Giant kelp blade detail with developing bryozoan colonies (whitish material), Santa Barbara Island.*

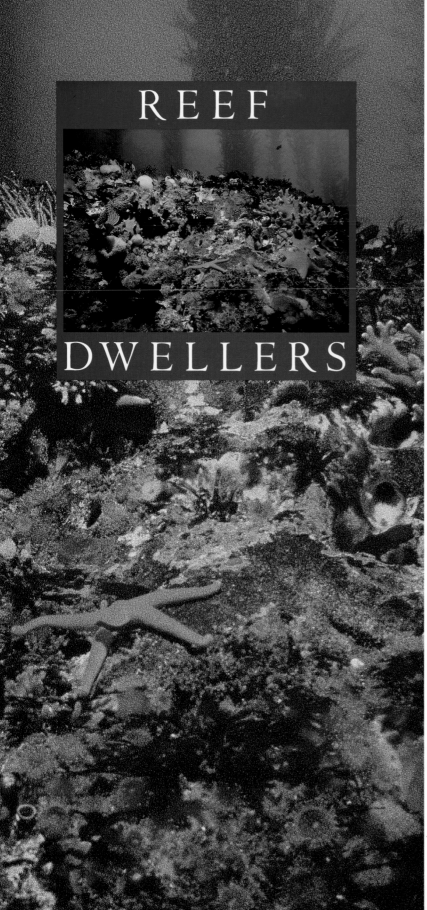

REEF
DWELLERS

It's ironic, indeed, that a rocky foundation that is neither animal nor vegetable, but mineral—and devoid of life—is of critical importance to a reef's size, shape, and the diversity and quantity of plants and animals it can support. California's reefs are supported by a variety of types of bedrock with different mineral compositions and physical contours. Rocky areas with deep cracks, crevices, and irregular surfaces provide the best substrate for attachment and attraction of fish and invertebrates. Conversely, flat uniform rock surfaces, sometimes called pavement rock, offer the least attractive surface area for plants and animals to live on and in. As a rule, the more irregular a rock surface is, the more life it can support.

Rocky pinnacles that approach or break the ocean's surface constitute an ideal reef design. They are also some of the most beautiful and exciting reefs to dive. Pinnacles can range in size from isolated rock mounds five or six feet high to mountainous structures looming one hundred feet or more out of the ocean bottom. Exposed on all sides to moving sea water, creatures that live on the steep walls of a pinnacle feast on waters that have not already been picked over by creatures farther down the coast. While kelp may only occupy a narrow area around the pinnacle's perimeter, the steep walls create a perfect environment for thick mats of colorful invertebrates such as anemones and pink, red, and purple hydrocorals.

Massive outcroppings of bedrock usually constitute the largest part of a reef's substrate, but large boulders, smaller cobblestone-sized rocks, and even layers of

PLATE 45. *Reef ledge detail with purple hydrocoral and seastars, Cypress Point, Carmel.*

PLATE 46. *Purple sea urchins with rock scallop shell, Santa Cruz Island.*

smaller gravel also contribute added surface area for housing marine life. While the harder minerals, such as volcanic basalt, serve as stronger attachment bases, smoother and more porous sandstone is easily bored into by marine organisms. Although this activity creates living space, the erosion caused by tunneling can weaken the bedrock and cause it to break away during storms or heavy wave activity.

On the reef, a life struggle between species for food and space is being waged. This competition is most readily seen in the giant kelp forest itself. A young kelp forest is typically composed of thinner kelp stalks, often between a few to a dozen stipes, tightly packed together. The young kelp stalks compete for space; eventually, reduction of light, limits on nutrients, and predation effectively thin out the forest. As the forest matures, the stalks thicken and hundreds of stipes may appear on each stalk. At this point, the kelp forest appears more open, and a diver can swim through it with less chance of snagging a tank or swim fins on the stalks.

Ecologists refer to well-developed terrestrial forests (ones that do not change much in human lifetimes) as climax communities. Climax communities are ones that tend to replace themselves when disturbed. A virgin spruce forest may be the result of thousands of years of what biologists term primary succession. The process of primary succession might have begun millennia ago after a volcanic explosion leveled the earth

PLATE 47. *Reef ledge with orange hydrocoral, Cypress Point, Carmel.*

PLATE 48. *Giant spined star with purple hydrocoral, Santa Barbara Island.*

PLATE 49. *Leafy hornmouth snail, Santa Catalina Island.*

PLATE 50. *Sea urchin test, Santa Catalina Island.*

47

48

49

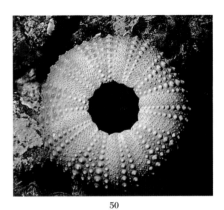

50

or perhaps after a glacier receded at the end of an ice age and left barren, pulverized earth in its wake. Wind-transported seeds fell on this bare rock; eventually the hardiest species took root. With the passing of time and the effect of weathering processes, soils slowly built up, allowing seeds that required milder growing conditions to germinate. As growing conditions improved, the seeds of light-tolerant trees such as oaks or alders took root; for a relatively short period of time these trees probably dominated the area in what is known as a subclimax forest. But the shade that these trees created, ironically, resulted in their demise by holding back sunlight from the forest floor. Shade-tolerant seeds such as spruce or hemlock germinated in their shadows and eventually dominated the forest, which became a climax community.

After a fire or other natural disaster that destroys part of the forest, some open space is created and a much faster reparation process called secondary succession begins. Again, shrubs and light-requiring trees settle in the open area, and again these species create shade and a suitable environment for the shade-tolerant hemlocks and spruces that eventually prevail.

The concept of biological succession also applies to a submerged reef, although the pattern of succession is not as well defined and the climax communities are not as dominant over time. On a well-developed reef in central and southern California, giant kelp usually dominates the reef from ten- to fifteen-foot depths, where wave activity limits kelp growth, to seventy to eighty feet, where reduced light levels limit the establishment of young sporophytes.

Upon close examination, though, it's apparent that

PLATE 51. *Spanish shawl nudibranch, Stern's Wharf, Santa Barbara.*

52

53

54

there is something for everybody in this complex community—from the tough neighborhoods within the surf zone, to the stony shadows beneath the giant kelp canopy, to the reef's deeper, dimly lit outer recesses.

Giant kelp is only one of some twenty species of kelp endemic to the California coastline. Although it is a hardy plant, its resilient stipes are no match for the constant battering of surf in very shallow water. Taking advantage of the giant kelp's limitations, hardier algae such as feather boa kelp, *Egregia laevigata*, have leathery fernlike blades that can withstand violent water movements; they thrive in shallow rocky waters at the reef's inner perimeter.

Somewhat akin to the shrubs and brush of a terrestrial forest, other brown algae, appropriately called understory kelps, compete for space in deeper water under the kelp canopy. These smaller plants, such as winged kelp, *Pterygophora californica*, and oarweed, *Laminaria farlowii*, fill the open spaces between giant kelp stalks. Usually intermingled among these understory kelps are a variety of other red, green, and brown algae such as rockweed, spongelike codium, and calcified coralline algae. In some areas, pink coralline algae covers vast areas of a reef ledge, lending it a reddish and quite beautiful hue. Collectively, these lush aggregations of seaweeds may completely cover the hard stony reef. Like a thick, vibrant, living carpet, they support a rich community of fish and invertebrates that finds refuge in the algae, feeds on it, or both.

In deeper waters on the reef's outer perimeter, lower light levels limit the giant kelp's growth. The limiting depth may be fifty to sixty feet or shallower in turbid water, or perhaps ninety to one hundred feet in areas where clear waters prevail. Beyond this demarcation line, other brown algae, such as bull kelp,

Nereocystis luetkeana, and elkhorn kelp, *Pelagophycus porra*, which have adapted to dim light, begin to take over the available spaces on the deep reef. (Bull kelp is most prevalent on the central California coast; elkhorn kelp is seen more on southern California reefs and farther south into Baja California.)

It is not clearly understood why the California reef climax community (at least in southern and central California) tends to culminate in a giant kelp forest habitat, especially when other hardy kelp species grow well under similar conditions. Each year, especially off the central California coast, winter storms may rip acres of giant kelp from the ocean bottom, leaving substantial areas of open reef. Immediately after such devastation, competition for space and survival begins. Newly exposed areas of bedrock are now suitable attachment sites for kelp spores, provided that other conditions for growth such as temperature, predation, and sedimentation are also favorable. (Sediment in the water reduces sunlight and hinders kelp growth; when it settles on the reef it can bury spores and prevent their attachment.)

Usually—perhaps because large numbers of giant kelp plants still surround the open reef areas, and there are more spores of that species floating down through the water column—*Macrocystis pyrifera* sporophytes begin to fill in the damaged areas, and the kelp forest repairs itself and endures.

A certain amount of luck, no doubt, is involved in

Plate 52. *Plume worms (also called "Christmas tree" worms), Santa Catalina Island.*

Plate 53. *Rainbow sea star skin pattern detail, Santa Cruz Island.*

Plate 54. *Giant spined star skin pattern detail, Santa Cruz Island.*

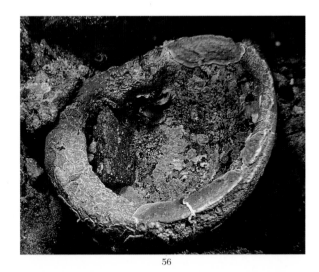

56

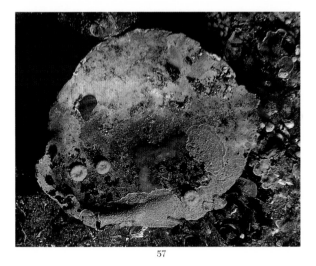

57

the reparation process. A winter storm also can be the catalyst that changes the dominant species of a reef. Sometimes, perhaps because less favorable conditions for giant kelp exist, understory kelps take over the open areas, creating shade and preventing giant kelp spores from germinating. In many areas of central California, the larger and very adaptable bull kelp is the dominant kelp species on exposed parts of the coast, surviving the same storms that wipe out stands of giant kelp.

Researchers studying some southern California reefs have noted four-year cycles: periods of giant kelp dominance followed by its thinning out or its complete disappearance and, later, the return of healthy thick kelp forests. Whether this cyclic phenomenon is a plan of nature, perhaps linked to El Niño, or the result of human pollution of local waters—or both—is not known for certain.

The cast of creatures occupying the kelp forest floor and its rocky caves and crevices is diverse and adaptive. For reasons of survival, they range from the garish to the obscure. The bright orange California garibaldi, *Hypsypops rubicundus,* is a classic example of the former. A member of the damselfish family, the garibaldi holds the distinction of being the only marine fish in California waters to be completely protected by state law from spearfishing and angling.

The garibaldi's bright coloration, which in the animal world sometimes proclaims, "Don't eat me, I don't taste good" or "Don't mistake me for another fish—I'm

PLATE 55. *Surfgrass, Cortez Bank.*

PLATE 56. *Abalone shell with coralline algae and plume worm, Santa Catalina Island.*

PLATE 57. *Rock scallop shell with orange cup corals and coralline algae, Santa Catalina Island.*

very territorial and will bite the living daylights out of you if you come too close," is perhaps what lends the pugnacious garibaldi its bold personality. It is fiercely territorial and will defend its home turf, which includes a shelter hole, feeding area, and breeding site, year round. Garibaldis have been known to protect the same territory for up to four or five years. Males are especially protective of their space on the reef during the breeding season, when they guard their egg-laden nests.

Male garibaldis cultivate their nests by clearing a rocky area of all debris and then installing a bed of live, filamentous red algae. The algae attach to the reef, forming a velvety soft covering over the rocky surface. Should any foreign material, such as a piece of kelpshed, for example, come to rest on the garibaldi's carefully crafted nest, the fish will grab it in its mouth, deposit it off to the side, and resume its guardpost. Once hatched, juveniles begin life with iridescent blue spots on their orange bodies. The spots gradually disappear as the fish reach adulthood.

Other fish on the reef live a more clandestine life. Nestled among clumps of algae on rock surfaces and in crevices, fish such as the snubnose sculpin, the painted greenling, and a variety of rockfish species have adpated to living much of their lives on or near the bottom. Their variously mottled skin patterns enable them to blend in with the reef's bottom coloration.

Rather than take risks with protective coloration,

PLATE 58. *Garibaldi, Santa Catalina Island.*

PLATE 59. *Blue-banded goby with plume worm, lavender Corynactis anemones, and bryozoans in foreground, Santa Catalina Island.*

PLATE 60. *Island kelpfish, Santa Catalina Island.*

PLATE 61 NEXT PAGE. *Garibaldis, Santa Barbara Island.*

59

60

62

other animals take up residence in crevices and caves deep within the reef. Often seen with just its head protruding from its rocky lair, the California moray eel is one such cave dweller. The moray's reputation as a toothy monster is undeserved; usually it is a docile, reclusive creature. When viewed up close at the entrance to its cave, the moray looks like an attack dog ready to bite, with its toothy jaws agape and flexed. (It is, in fact, pumping water over its gills.) Divers have hand fed morays, and photographers have taken their portraits from close quarters without mishap. (It would be foolish to reach blindly into any reef cave lest a frightened moray strike out in self defense.)

Also living in these caves and crevices, often cohabiting with the moray, are rock shrimp and California spiny lobsters. Some shrimp live in a symbiotic relationship with the moray. The shrimp picks food particles out of the moray's teeth: in exchange for a meal, the moray enjoys good dental health. While seldom seen on the open reef by day, the spiny lobster, like many other crustaceans, emerges from its cave at night to feed in protective darkness.

Along the reef's top and sides, every nook, cranny, and open surface has been occupied or encrusted by plants and animals. Sometimes what appears to be vegetable is also animal. Sporting a hubcap-shaped shell often heavily encrusted with algae and other invertebrates, the California abalone is another resident of the rocky reef ledge. Eight species of abalone inhabit California waters. A mollusk, the abalone is a member of the same phylum of animals as snails, clams, and

the octopus. The abalone's flattened, disk-shaped shell is suited to the turbulent waters it inhabits and to the tight crevices where it hides. An herbivore, the abalone maneuvers across rocky surfaces feasting on reef algae; when alarmed, it clamps its muscular foot to the bottom, which makes its removal extremely difficult. (This same foot muscle, which affords the abalone protection in its habitat, has also caused it to be a valuable item in California's fishery. When cut into thin slices and tenderized, this foot muscle becomes abalone steak, a popular gourmet delicacy.) Because of pollution and overfishing, abalone are difficult if not impossible to find on mainland reefs, especially in southern California. They still inhabit reefs bordering offshore islands that are farther removed from fishing pressure and the effects of coastal sewage disposal, which, especially in southern California, has reduced the kelp habitat and, as a result, the abalone's source of food.

Farther down the side of a ledge and under the reef's rocky overhang, a drastic transition of life forms takes place. Here, another community of animals and plants forms thick mats. Unlike the creatures that inhabit the uppermost sunlit regions of the reef, those that live under the reef's ledges in relative darkness enjoy a life free from the encroachment of kelp and other algae that thrive in sunlight.

PLATE 62. *Hermit crab inside wavy top snail shell, Santa Catalina Island.*

PLATE 63. *California moray eel, San Clemente Island.*

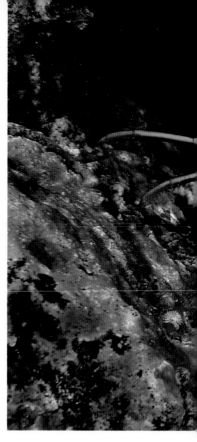

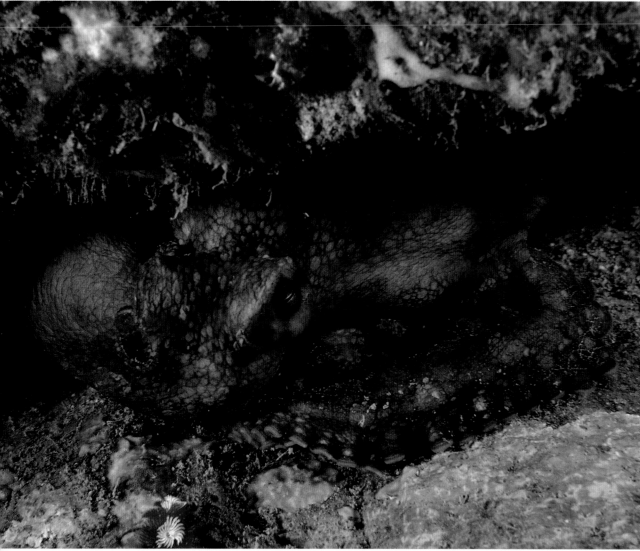

65

66

A saturation of rainbow-bright life hides in these shadows. Some ledges glow with the color of thousands of club anemones, *Corynactis californica.* While the club anemone can be found in deep areas as well as shallow intertidal waters from Sonoma County to Santa Barbara, it is temperature sensitive and grows in progressively deeper waters southward; in the La Jolla submarine canyon it grows as deep as ninety to one hundred feet. These deep colonies of *Corynactis* commonly seen under reef ledge overhangs create a spectacular assemblage of color. In deeper waters where the ocean's selective color absorption removes the red, orange, and yellow wave lengths of light, the club anemone exhibits a vivid fluorescence.

Sometimes called the club anemone because of its club-shaped tentacles, *Corynactis* has the ability to reproduce both sexually and asexually. Asexual reproduction takes place by longitudinal fission: the animal splits evenly down the middle and forms an exact mirror image of itself. Offspring formed in this manner are always the same color and are joined to their parent at the basal disk. Dense mats of these interconnected individuals can form on hard substrates, but they cannot adhere to sand or loose sediment.

In contrast, sexual reproduction gives rise to drifting larvae that can begin life at a distance from the parent colony. Thus, the club anemone enjoys reproductive double indemnity: the asexual mode results in large aggregations, whereas the sexual mode assures dispersal of the species.

Like all anemones, the club anemone is a member

PLATE 64. *Octopus in rocky lair, Santa Catalina Island.*

PLATE 65. *California spiny lobster, San Clemente Island.*

PLATE 66. *Island kelpfish, Santa Catalina Island.*

of the phylum Cnidaria. Cnidarians are equipped with special stinging cells in their tentacles called *nematocysts*, which fire when prey brushes up against them. The anemone envelops its prey—which range from small fish or plankton to organic particles—and pulls the food into its mouth with its tentacles.

The painted greenling has a symbiotic relationship with the club anemone. By acclimating the mucus on its skin to the anemone colony, it swims freely around, nestles into, and rests among the anemone's deadly tentacles without being stung. The greenling thus lures other unsuspecting fish into the anemone's stinging cells while enjoying bodyguard service.

While the painted greenling has a harmonious relationship with the anemone, some members of the Mollusk phylum called *nudibranchs*, or sea slugs, prey on the tentacles of anemones and their relatives, the hydroids. Nudibranchs are closely related to snails, but they have lost their shells and display lobe-shaped rows of gills, called *cerata*, or smaller gill plumes, on their dorsal surface.

PLATE 67. *White-spotted rose anemone, Mono Lobo Point, Monterey.*

PLATE 68. *Giant green anemone, San Nicolas Island.*

PLATE 69. *Orange cup coral, San Clemente Island.*

PLATE 70 NEXT PAGE. *Club anemone, Stern's Wharf, Santa Barbara.*

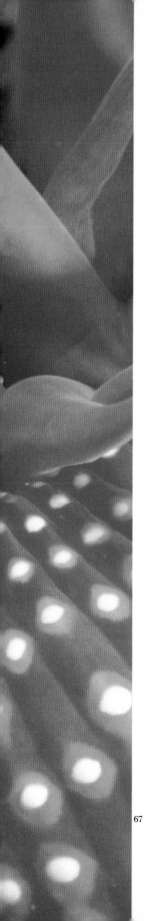

68

67

69

While some nudibranchs are drab, most are vibrant, like the purple-and-orange Spanish shawl. Nudibranchs prey on the stinging cells of anemones and hydroids and can pass them through their digestive tract without causing the deadly stinging cells to fire. They then absorb the stinging cells into their cerata, using them for their own defense. While the nudibranch's garish coloration and borrowed stinging cells provide an effective defense, at least one predator, the carnivorous *Navanax* nudibranch, is undeterred and is a specialist at devouring other nudibranchs.

If only a creature is willing and able to adapt, life on the reef is a moveable feast.

PLATE 71. *Spanish shawl nudibranch, Anacapa Island.*

PLATE 72. *Horned nudibranch on bryozoans, San Nicolas Island.*

PLATE 73. *Rose anemone, Mono Lobo Point, Monterey.*

71

72

73

ON THE
OUTER EDGE

Swimming from a rocky ledge with its dense concentration of plants and animals to the sandy plain adjacent to the reef at first seems like traveling from an oasis to a desert.

Whether in the sandy channels that separate sections of the rocky reef or on the vast sandy plains that stretch for miles on the outer edge of the kelp forest, life on the sandy bottom pales by comparison to the lush communities that cling to the reef's ledges or find sanctuary within the kelp stalks and other seaweeds.

The sandy bottom, though, is only lifeless by comparison. Closer inspection reveals a community of specialized creatures adept at digging, hiding, and making use of what may in large part be waste products and debris from the neighboring rocky reef and open ocean.

These sandy areas often lie shoreward on the inside boundary of the rocky reef, within channels that cut across the reef, or seaward on the reef's outer edge. A swim through the surf zone, across the reef, and into deep water reveals that all sands are not the same: shallow and deep waters offer separate challenges to marine life living on the soft bottom.

Existence in a sand environment in shallow waters is arduous at best. Wave surge and longshore currents are strongest here. The shifting sands leave animals in a perilous state of flux: they must survive while being alternately buried and exposed by the moving bottom. Suspended sand, churned by wave action, is abrasive to marine life and to the rock surfaces that border sandy regions, preventing settlement of life on these otherwise suitable surfaces.

Creatures that endure on the sandy bottom in shal-

PLATE 74. *Jack mackerel, Santa Catalina Island.*

PLATE 75. *Pacific angel shark eye detail, Santa Cruz Island.*

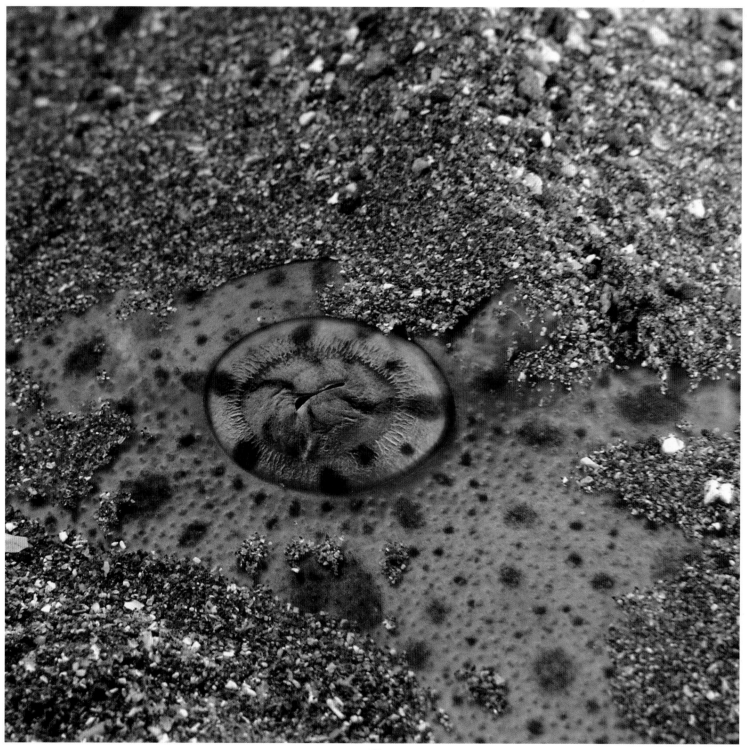

75

76

77

low turbulent waters are either excellent diggers or able to uncover and mobilize themselves when necessary. Tube-building worms, clams, spiny sand stars, and sand dollars do well here. Some species of clams are proficient diggers and live out their life filter-feeding just beyond the surf zone, with only their two incurrent and excurrent siphons protruding through the sand surface. Tube worms combine sand grains with body secretions to form stuccolike tubes that extend three inches or more below the bottom, thus forming a protective subterranean shelter into which they can withdraw from predators. Tube worms feed with ciliated tentacles that extend symmetrically outward several centimeters; they consume detritus and other water-borne particles that settle on their sticky tentacles by drawing them into centrally located mouths. Large numbers of tube worms living in close proximity to each other perform a community service by stabilizing the bottom and reducing sand movement. This eases the stress on other sand-dwelling creatures.

The sandy plains adjacent to the reef in deeper waters from forty to one hundred twenty feet present a milder environment that is less affected by wave action or moving sand. In shallow water, wave action keeps lighter, finer sands in suspension, leaving coarser sand on the nearshore bottom. In deeper water, where there is less wave surge, finer sands and silts remain on the bottom. In waters eighty to one hundred twenty feet deep where the wave surge is least, a thin slurry of detritus, algal remnants, and other minute particles coats the sand. This organic material, which drifts down from the rocky reef or

PLATE 76. *Channeled nassa, Monterey.*

PLATE 77. *Wavy turban snail encrusted with coralline algae, Santa Catalina Island.*

falls from the open water above, offers a benthic smorgasbord to creatures such as small white sea urchins, brittle stars, tube worms, sea pens, and tube anemones.

Armies of vibrantly colored bat stars—red, orange, lavender, and multicolored—decorate the sand bottom in places. Sometimes a large ball of bat stars envelops a decaying fish carcass in a slow-motion feeding frenzy easily mistaken for an echinoderm wrestling match or an undersea orgy.

The brilliantly colored bat stars advertise their presence. Close by, in stark contrast, stealthy pairs of eyes protrude above the sand where flatfish such as speckled sand dabs, California halibut, bat rays, and angel sharks lie hidden. These well-camouflaged predators rely on protective coloration and their ability to bury themselves in the sand to trick unsuspecting prey, which include anchovies, other small fish, and crustaceans and mollusks.

The web of predators and prey that seems complex and overwhelming on the rocky reef is well defined here on the sandy plains. In the waters above the sand bottom, just as in the kelp forest, currents bathe the area in a rich planktonic soup. Free floating and largely at the mercy of wind and currents for locomotion, these microscopic creatures constitute the very beginning of the oceanic food chain and the nutritional foundation of life in the sea. Plant plankton, or *phytoplankton*, are mixed in a life-sustaining broth with animal plankton, or *zooplankton*. Phytoplankton are

PLATE 78. *Bat stars, Monterey.*

PLATE 79. *Bat stars with nudibranch egg ribbon, Monterey.*

PLATE 80. *Bat star skin pattern detail, Lovers' Cove, Monterey.*

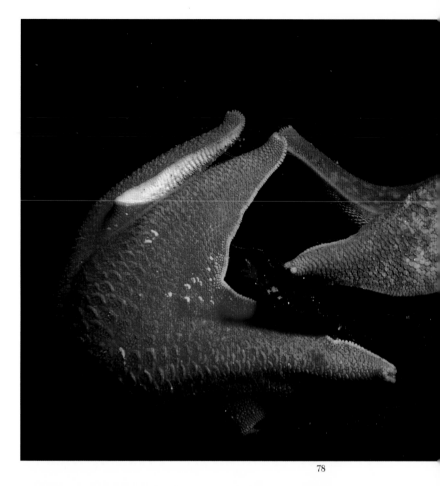

78

79

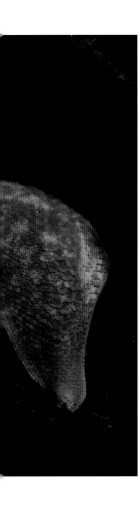

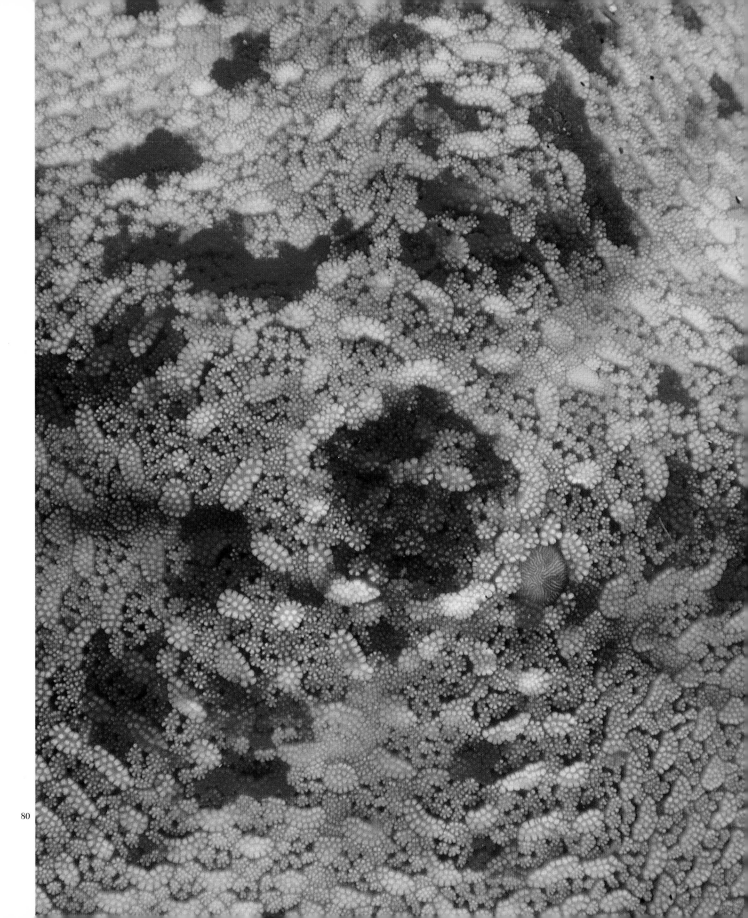

80

actually the ocean's primary producers and are comprised largely of two types—diatoms and dinoflagellates. Although they are tiny plants, diatoms look like creatures from outer space when viewed under a microscope. Their golden-brown interiors are covered with glass-walled casings, some like pillboxes, others forming spiked chains. Dinoflagellates look equally foreign upon close inspection but have an appendage for locomotion called a flagellum.

Zooplankton may be the larval forms of fish or invertebrates that are living a short, temporary free-floating existence before developing into larger animals, or they may remain buglike microscopic crustaceans throughout their entire lives.

PLATE 81. *Blackeye goby on orange bat star, Monterey.*

82

83

84

Other larger animals such as sardines and anchovies feed on zooplankton; in turn, predators such as barracuda, halibut, and lingcod consume these small fish. Later these fish may be pursued by a variety of even larger predators, such as seals and sea lions or, perhaps, the rays and sharks that cruise California waters, such as blues, makos, and even great whites.

Sometimes animals choose to omit the middlemen in the hierarchy of the reef food web and feast directly upon plankton. Reaching reported lengths of thirty to forty feet, the basking shark is one of these. A seasonal visitor, the basking shark shows up off the southern California coast in fall and early winter and off the central coast in spring and summer. Although its dorsal fin, tail fin, grayish coloration, and huge girth sometimes cause it to be mistaken for its more toothy relative the great white, which also inhabits local waters, the basking shark has very small teeth (about five millimeters long) and filter-feeds using specialized gill rakers that form a sievelike mesh in its throat. Ironically, this shark, the world's second-largest fish next to the whale shark, survives by preying directly on the sea's very smallest inhabitants.

Unlike the rocky reef, which, at least in human terms, appears somewhat the same from day to day, the midwater area above the sandy plains on the reef's outer edge can change drastically from one day to another—and even from one hour to next.

A dive in open water on the reef's outer edge is always a gamble, with the odds stacked in favor of an uneventful swim in emerald-green waters. Now

PLATE 82. *Twenty-foot-long basking shark, feeding, Santa Barbara Channel near Carpenteria.*

PLATE 83. *Pacific angel shark, Santa Catalina Island.*

PLATE 84. *Blue shark, near Santa Cruz Island.*

85

and again, though, a diver's patience is rewarded when a school of jack mackerel emerges like lightning out of the liquid horizon. As they zoom past, pulsating in unison and making silvery reflections, a school of barracuda follows in hot pursuit. The encounter may last just fifteen or twenty seconds before the bait fish are chased shoreward into the protection of the kelp forest. Then the underwater horizon, having changed from a void to a saturation of life and energy, changes back again, all within half a minute.

On other days during late fall and early winter, pods of California gray whales cruise past. A lone individual lingers outside the kelp line as fellow whales migrate south from subarctic feeding grounds in Alaska to breeding and calving lagoons in Baja California; their ten-thousand-mile roundtrip voyage is believed to be the longest migration undertaken by any mammal.

Sometimes, when reproductive conditions are especially favorable in a far-off part of the sea, winds and currents sweep large numbers of ocean drifters close to the California coast. What those creatures will be and when they will arrive is an unknown that makes diving on the reef's outer edge and farther out into blue water intriguing. During the most recent El Niño, for example, large aggregations of pelagic red crabs, *Pleuroncodes planipes*, also called squat lobsters or tuna crabs, temporarily invaded coastal waters by the millions. Normally inhabiting tropical waters, this species is associated with and preyed upon by tuna,

usually farther south off Mexico and Central and South America. In some places, such as the Monterey harbor area, for example, the tuna crab invasion was so intense that these three- to four-inch-long crustaceans were piled a foot deep on the beaches, pushed there by waves and tides. Local rooftops were soon decorated with pink guano from hungry gulls taking full advantage of this gift from nature.

At other times of the year, the open ocean may send large concentrations of jellyfish and long gelatinous chains of vertebrate animals called *salps* close to the California coast. On the outer edge of the reef at these times, ocean sunfish venture close to shore to feast on jellyfish, while señoritas leave the protection of the kelp forest to nibble on the huge salp colonies or to clean parasites off cooperative sunfish that rest quietly near the ocean surface while the bucktoothed señoritas pick away at pests on their epidermis.

Swimming on the surface in small groups called pods, California sea lions, *Zalophus californianus*, are frequent visitors to the outside edge of the reef. They will take full advantage of these unusual conditions to munch on lethargic sunfish, biting off their fins and playing with the carcass like cats with a dead mouse.

PLATE 85. *Sand dollar, Monterey.*

PLATE 86. *Bat star with tube anemone, Monterey.*

PLATE 87 NEXT PAGE. *California halibut, off Cannery Row, Monterey.*

Opportunistic eaters like sea lions forage within the kelp forest as well as in deeper waters. They use their incredible swimming ability, sharp teeth, and keen eyesight to chase down their main diet of fish and squid. Foraging both day and night, with no regular feeding pattern, sea lions are capable of lightning-quick bursts of speed underwater and can dive in excess of one hundred eighty feet.

It's hard to not anthropomorphize when diving with sea lions. Their insatiable curiosity and amusing antics have endeared them to California divers, who sometimes refer to them as clowns of the sea. It is not uncommon when diving near a sea lion rookery to be dive-bombed by a pod of sea lions that veers off at the last instant. From a human standpoint, it seems a game designed to make the diver flinch. They don't intend to cause physical harm (except, perhaps, for drowning by laughter). Sea lions seem fascinated by diving hardware and software. More than once they have chewed on my swim fins and regulator hoses. Once I felt a yank and almost lost both snorkel and mask when a pup tried to swim away with its newfound toys.

Both sea lions and harbor seals, *Phoca vitulina*, inhabit California waters. The two are often mistaken for each other when viewed from above water. There is absolutely no mistaking them, however, underwater.

Sea lions and harbor seals are both members of the suborder Pinnipedia ("feather-feet"), which also includes fur seals and walruses. Sea lions and harbor seals differ markedly in their body structure, swim-

PLATE 88. *Molted rock crab shell, Point Lobos at Whalers' Cove, Carmel.*

PLATE 89. *Pelagic red crab, Santa Catalina Island.*

PLATE 90. *Pelagic red crab silhouette, Santa Catalina Island.*

88

89

90

ming style, and coloration. Aside from their dark fur, small external ears, a longer neck, and a more slender, torpedo-shaped body, sea lions have notably different swimming appendages. Their front flippers are larger in relation to their body size and they can erect their rear fins to aid in terrestrial locomotion. Harbor seals are unable to right their rear flippers. They also have lighter-colored fur with dark spots. In contrast to the fur-covered fins of harbor seals, sea lion fins are covered with a dark pigmented skin.

When swimming, sea lions use their well-developed chest muscles and foreflippers to propel themselves, employing their rear flippers as a steering rudder. Harbor seals swim primarily with their hind appendages.

On a calm day on the outer edge, I have surfaced many times outside the kelp line, with the reef sandwiched between the open sea and the mountains of the Coast Range looming out of the distant shoreline.

PLATE 91. *California sea lions, Santa Barbara Island.*

91

93

If you listen closely you can sometimes hear the soft whir of automobile tires scurrying along the long asphalt ribbons of the Pacific Coast Highway and the Ventura Freeway.

For me, this is always an enlightening moment, a moment that emphasizes an important Gaian attachment of land and sea. Floating peacefully and freely without moving a muscle, you can snorkel on the ocean surface just outside the kelp line and literally, if only briefly, be planktonic. As you rock in a gentle swell, breathing quietly through a rubber air tube, the miraculousness and universality of this amazing ecosystem overcomes you while sunlight dances through the water, illuminating tiny planktonic specks that sparkle like stars.

If you turn your gaze landward across hundreds of yards of floating kelp toward the cloud-topped mountains, you can see how the land and sea nurture each other in a delicate balancing act of energy and nutrients. Water vapor evaporates from the ocean and rises into the atmosphere to form clouds that later rain on the earth; rivers and streams pour off the land, sending minerals, salts, and organic matter rushing to the nearshore environment. Soon, the coastal ocean receives this bounty and uses sunlight to convert it into plant and animal life—even the waste products and dead remains of reef life become nutrients that are consumed by the reef or that drift into deeper water, eventually to be recycled by the ocean's upwelling.

PLATE 92. *California sea lions, Santa Barbara Island.*

PLATE 93. *Tube anemone, Monterey.*

The cycle of life—the circle of life—continues here as it has for thousands of years. If we know nothing else, we know that we are just one part of this delicately balanced and vulnerable community. But we are a part that can have a tremendous impact. We can allow vast areas of pristine undersea terrain to be silted over by insufficiently treated sewage, tainted by illegally dumped toxics, and over- and improperly fished. Or we can guard our coastal reefs and treat them as the state treasure they truly are, for the care we extend to our coastal marine environment we really extend to ourselves. What flows to the sea in a river or stream—or sewer—ultimately becomes part of the sea, part of the plankton, part of the fish, and part of us. Just as the sea cannot be divorced from the land nor the earth from the cosmos, we, and California reefs, are all connected.

PLATE 94. *Spiny sand star, Santa Rosa Island.*

PLATE 95. *Blacksmith, Santa Catalina Island.*

94

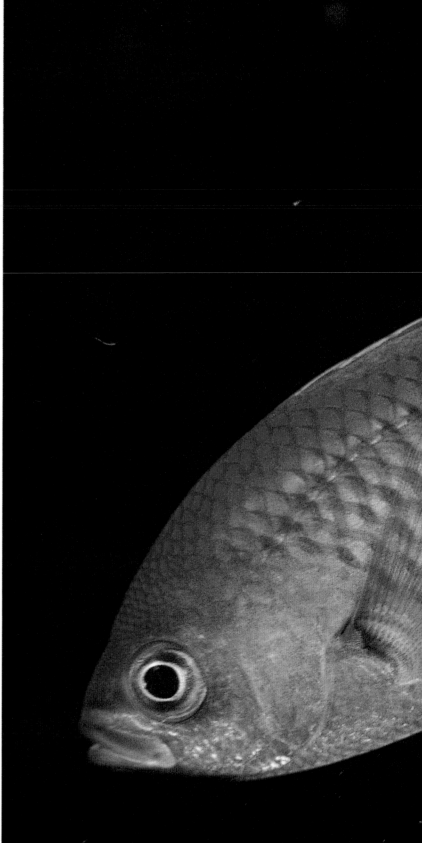

95

GLOSSARY

Included in the following glossary are prominent terms used throughout the text and captions. In some cases the terms have already been briefly explained in the text but are defined here in greater depth. Terms used only once in the text—and well defined at that point—have not been included.

algae — Primitive, single- or multicellular plants; primarily aquatic, such as the seaweeds.

algin — Substance found in marine brown algae, especially giant kelp; used chiefly as a stabilizing, emulsifying, thickening, coating, or water-holding agent in foods (such as ice cream) and commercial products.

anemone — *See* sea anemone

apical tip — Specialized, actively growing tip of a giant kelp blade from which other blades and bladders (pneumatocysts) develop.

benthic — Living on or near the bottom of the ocean.

biological succession — Process by which communities of plants and animals succeed each other until a stable, "climax" state is reached.

bladder — Gas-filled float that gives buoyancy to kelp and other seaweeds.

blade — Leaflike plant appendage.

bottom surge — Horizontal oscillation of water near the ocean bottom resulting from surface wave action.

bryozoans — Microscopic aquatic animals that live in colonies on rocks or seaweeds. Also called moss animals because some of their colonies are delicately branched and resemble seaweed; other colonies form thin lacy encrustations.

calcareous — Containing calcium carbonate.

canopy — Upper growth of a giant kelp forest; often floats in dense mats on the ocean surface, shading the sea bed below.

Cnidaria — Large, diverse group of saclike invertebrate animals including sea anemones, corals, hydroids, and jellyfish. Cnidarians have a tubular digestive cavity with a single opening surrounded by tentacles containing stinging cells called nematocysts, which are used to capture prey. The body of cnidarians is radially symmetrical, like the spokes of a wheel; it may either be attached to the ocean bottom or some other substrate in polyp form, like the sea anemone, or float freely in medusa form, like the jellyfish.

colloidal — Gelatinous.

coralline algae — Group of red algae that absorbs calcium carbonate from seawater to form chalky cell walls. Coralline algae may grow either in hard, brittle encrusting forms on rock or in more flexible erect, branchlike forms attached to a solid substrate.

corals — Cnidarian polyps that secrete protective skeletons. Like other cnidarians, corals have tentacles armed with stinging cells, or nematocysts.

Coriolis effect Apparent force resulting from the earth's rotation that deflects winds and moving water to the right in the Northern Hemisphere and to the left in the Southern Hemisphere.

crustacean Large class of marine and freshwater arthropods—segmented animals with an external skeleton—including barnacles, shrimp, crabs, and lobsters.

detritus Dead organic material and the live microscopic organisms associated with its decomposition.

echinoderms "Spiny-skinned" group of marine invertebrates with a supporting skeleton within the skin (an endoskeleton) composed of calcium carbonate plates. These plates may be loosely joined, as in sea stars; fused to form a rigid shell, or test, as in sea urchins; or greatly reduced so that the animal has a soft, fleshy appearance, as in sea cucumbers.

ecosystem In nature, an interactive unit of living and nonliving parts that exchange materials in a circular path to produce a stable system. Any ecosystem has four components: producers, consumers, decomposers, and the nonliving environment. Components of the marine ecosystem include the living and nonliving parts of streams, rivers, the land they flow across, and the ocean they empty into.

filter feeding Feeding technique used by some marine animals, such as sponges, clams, tube worms, sea anemones, and baleen whales, to filter plankton and other small organic matter from a current of water passing through specialized parts of their bodies.

food chain Series of organisms through which energy is transferred by feeding. Each organism eats the preceding one in the sequence and is in turn eaten by another further up the chain. Green plants are at the bottom of the food chain and obtain their energy through photosynthesis.

food web All the interconnected food chains in a natural community.

frond Structure growing from a giant kelp holdfast; consists of a stemlike stipe, leaflike blades, and bladders that provide flotation.

gorgonians Colorful soft corals that secrete a flexible inner skeleton composed in part of a horny substance called gorgonin. Commonly called sea fans, gorgonians look like beautiful underwater plants.

haptera Branching rootlike strands that anchor a kelp plant to the substrate.

holdfast Conical assemblage of haptera at the base of a kelp plant that firmly secures it to the substrate.

hydrocorals Colonial corals that secrete an often brightly colored external calcareous skeleton. Hydrocorals may form either encrusting or upright branching colonies.

intertidal waters Area along the coast between mean high-water and mean low-water levels; also called the littoral zone.

invertebrate Animal without a spinal column or backbone.

kelp Large brown algae.

kelp line Generally, the shoreward or seaward surface boundary of a giant kelp forest as evidenced by the floating kelp canopy, or "mat."

kelpshed Aging, dying, or damaged kelp fronds that have fallen or drifted to the kelp forest floor.

kelpwrack Dying or damaged kelp that has been pushed ashore by waves, winds, or currents. After severe winter storms, tons of kelpwrack may appear on beaches as a single rubbery, twisted mass.

mammal Vertebrate animal characterized by hair and mammary glands that produce milk to nurse offspring. All mammals have lungs, breathe air, bear live young, and are warm blooded.

marine mammal Mammals such as whales, dolphins, seals, sea lions, walruses, otters, and manatees that spend part or all of their lives in the ocean.

mollusk Invertebrate animal with a soft unsegmented body consisting of a head and a muscular foot for movement. Most mollusks, such as abalone, clams, oysters, and mussels, are covered by a hard shell. Others, such as sea hares and nudibranchs, are "naked."

nudibranch Marine mollusk closely related to snails but lacking an external shell. Also known as sea slugs, nudibranchs appear in a wide variety of forms and colors.

opportunistic Feeding on a wide variety of organisms with no set feeding pattern.

pelagic Pertaining to or living in the open ocean.

photosynthesis Process by which green plants use solar energy to convert carbon dioxide and water into the chemical energy of sugars.

phylum Largest classification category of the animal kingdom; members of the same phylum are assumed to have a common ancestry.

plankton Free-floating aquatic life forms that are often (but not necessarily) microscopic in size and have limited means of locomotion. Plankton are generally distributed at the mercy of wind and currents. Planktonic plants are known as phytoplankton; planktonic animals are called zooplankton.

pneumatocysts Gas-filled bladders or floats that give buoyancy to giant kelp and other marine algae.

pod Number of animals (such as seals, sea lions, or whales) closely clustered together.

polyp Form of cnidarians that is attached to the ocean bottom or other substrate.

sea anemone   Fleshy, cylindrical marine animal with a tubelike hollow gut surrounded by flowerlike tentacles. Anemones attach to rocks, pilings, or kelp or burrow in sand or mud. When feeding, they paralyze their prey with specialized stinging cells called nematocysts, then fold their tentacles inward, drawing their food with them.

sea urchin   Hedgehoglike echinoderm characterized by external spines and a hard spherical shell, or test, composed of fused calcium carbonate plates.

seaweed   General term for marine algae.

sporophylls   Narrow, specialized reproductive blades that produce spores on giant kelp; located just above the holdfast.

sporophyte   Adult generation of giant kelp plant; produces spores.

stipe   Stemlike part of giant kelp plant that emerges from the haptera of the holdfast and with its assemblage of blades and bladders forms a frond.

substrate   Surface upon which plants and animals attach.

symbiotic relationship   A close nutritional relationship between two different species of organisms. The relationship may benefit both species or only one.

test   In sea urchins, the calcium carbonate shell that protects the soft internal body parts and supports the spines.

tide   Cyclic rise and fall of the ocean along the coast.

tube worm   Marine worm that lives in a self-secreted tube.

turbidity   Cloudiness; muddiness.

vertebrate   Animal with a spinal column or backbone.

wave surge   *See* bottom surge.

Appendix I

UNDERWATER PHOTOGRAPHY

The hundreds of hours I spent photographing underwater off the California coast in pursuit of the images for *California Reefs* have been some of the most memorable and enjoyable hours of my life. To a casual observer watching me prepare to embark on one of my undersea sorties, however, I might understandably be considered a masochist for making such a statement.

Photographing underwater is always a labor of love for me, but it would be misleading to say that the process does not involve a great deal of physical labor and tedium as well. Underwater photography requires (in addition to water, of course) diving ability, patience, tenacity, and lots of equipment. And most of the latter, unfortunately, is bulky and heavy.

Before each photographic outing, depending on where I'm shooting, hours of preparation are usually required to ready the arsenal of cameras, housings, strobes, light meters, and mounting brackets that are required for me to make underwater pictures. Each must be meticulously cleaned, loaded, and test-fired, and packed in a carrying case for its journey to the shore or onto a dive boat.

My diving equipment is checked and packed with almost as much ritualistic paranoia as my cameras. Following a mental checklist that has evolved over many years of diving, I begin by zipping open a large nylon duffel bag and tossing it flat on the floor. Fins, masks (I always pack two, just in case), snorkel, and dive knife go in first—fins flat on the bottom to protect the mask faceplates—then exposure suit (either a dry suit or wet suit) and accessories such as gloves and boots. My breathing regulator comes next, but before sandwiching it in between the rubber folds of my diving suit, I first mount it on a scuba bottle to test-breathe it and check its submersible pressure gauge. Decompression tables and decompression meter as well as a small watertight tool box for making infield repairs on diving and camera equipment go into a large zippered side pocket on the same duffel. Finally, in the same pocket I also pack an even smaller spare-parts kit with extra mask and fin straps, tank O-rings (neoprene or silicon seals that make an air/watertight seal between the breathing regulator and tank valve), and a list of phone numbers to call for diving-related accidents or emergencies.

With most of my dive gear packed, I pull out a couple of tank backpacks (harnesses that allow a diving tank to be worn on the back) and anywhere from two to six scuba bottles and check that they are completely filled with compressed air. Finally, I add a lead weight belt that may weigh anywhere from fourteen to twenty pounds, if I'm going to wear a wet suit, or thirty pounds if I'm using a dry suit. I usually also carry a few extra two- and three-pound lead weights to make small adjustments to my weight belt.

Ironically, with the exception of how much film and clothing I bring with me, the amount of equipment required for a one-day dive trip is about the same as that needed for an expedition of one or two weeks. And once the equipment is prepared and packed, it usually has to be handled several times as it is loaded into a car or truck, transported to the shore, and often handled again from the waterfront to the pier and onto a boat. Whether my diving expedition is simply a day trip to one of the offshore islands aboard a charter boat out of San Pedro or a ten-day excursion to the central California coast, one axiom remains: all equipment carried down to the sea must later be carried back again. It is usually a surprising and little-known fact to most people that the greatest amount of physical exertion in diving and photographing underwater is simply in relocating so much equipment to and from the dive site. For me, the diving part is easy by comparison.

DIVING SKILLS AND EQUIPMENT

All of the photographs in this book were taken while using scuba gear (*self-contained underwater breathing apparatus*). In discussing underwater photographic technique, the very first and most vital item to consider is the diver's own diving abilities. It is impossible here to include an in-depth discussion on diving techniques—volumes have been written on the subject. I will, however, touch lightly on a few of the most important points as they relate to underwater photography for those readers who may already be trained divers or who may be contemplating enrollment in one of the many diving certification programs available through most dive shops.

To photograph successfully underwater, one must be totally at home in the water and have mastered all diving techniques and equipment so that clearing the water out of a partially flooded face mask or making a quick adjustment on a tank or weight belt strap can be done easily and automatically, almost without thinking about it—while still holding onto a camera housing that may have two strobes attached to it. Successful underwater photography especially demands that a diver develop near-perfect buoyancy skills.

Underwater buoyancy can be controlled by adjusting the amount of lead weight worn on the diver's weight belt or by using a buoyancy control device,

usually worn on the diver's torso or tank. Sometimes it's desirable to have a slight negative buoyancy—that is, to be heavier than the water—for instance, while shooting on the bottom in moderate surge. At other times, such as when swimming through the open spaces of a kelp forest or in blue water on the outer edge of a reef, the diver may need neutral buoyancy—that is, to remain at the same depth, neither sinking nor rising. Throughout a day of diving (especially when using a wet suit), I will make small adjustments to my weight belt to compensate for my diving depth. If I'm working in a hundred feet of water, I may only wear fourteen pounds, because seawater pressure compresses the neoprene wet suit rubber and makes it more negatively buoyant at depth, but as I work in progressively shallower water, later in the day, I will add small amounts of weight. Late in the day I may find myself working in twenty or thirty feet of water and wearing twenty or more pounds on my belt so that I will have slightly negative buoyancy while working in a moderate bottom surge. (When a diver is making several dives in a day, nitrogen bubbles accumulating in the blood shorten diving time on each subsequent dive—the deeper, the shorter. Thus it is considered safer diving technique to do the deepest dives first and then work progressively shallower.)

Buoyancy can also be fine tuned by the breath. With a full breath of air, a diver will tend to remain at the same depth or very slowly begin to rise; upon exhaling, the diver will begin to very slowly sink. It is imperative, however, that a diver *never* hold his or her breath while ascending because the air trapped in the lungs will expand and cause serious lung injury.

Proper buoyancy is a necessity in obtaining good

photographs and is even more important in preventing damage to the reef. An overweighted diver, kicking fiercely to maintain position with a camera, can in one sweeping fin-kick wipe out several square feet of fragile hydrocoral or other delicate reef life that may take years to regenerate. Taking care not to let diving hardware such as dangling pressure gauge hoses and consoles drag along the reef and being careful as to where hands, elbows, and knees are braced when photographing will also help minimize reef damage.

It is difficult to accomplish the technical and creative tasks of picture making if you are shivering and nearly hypothermic. Even during the middle of summer, California water temperatures are chilly at normal diving depths. A well-fitting neoprene wet suit is the first choice of most California divers for minimum protection against the elements. For most of my diving I prefer a full quarter-inch wet suit with farmer John–style bottoms and a pullover jacket. The entire suit is constructed of smooth "skin-in" neoprene on the inside (for warmth and flexibility) and is nylon coated on the exterior for ease of wear. My suit was custom made by the West Suit Factory in Santa Barbara and has only one zipper, in the chest, as zippers are entry points for seawater to circulate and reduce the warmth of a wet suit. I also wear a diving hood that is sewn into the jacket, which further reduces water circulation and increases warmth. The suit has separate hard-sole boots, and I generally wear eighth-inch neoprene five-fingered gloves as well.

In recent years, during the dead of winter in southern California when I must make several long dives per day or when I'm working north of Point Conception off the central California coast, where the water is much cooler, I've opted to use a dry suit. My choice of dry suits is the DUI CF200X/SP model manufactured by Diving Unlimited International of San Diego, which I believe to be one of the best available. Dry suits have a watertight zipper and seals in the neck, wrist, and sometimes in the ankles that prevent seawater from entering. By wearing an insulating undergarment beneath the dry suit, the diver can stay substantially warmer than in a wet suit. Although dry suits are definitely bulkier, more expensive, and demand more maintenance, there is simply no comparison to the added comfort that I believe quite simply translates into better photographs.

The last thing an underwater photographer should have to worry about when photographing undersea is where the next breath of air is coming from. To this end, I find it convenient to mount all of my gauges on a console that can be quickly scanned with the flick of the wrist to determine depth, bottom time, and remaining air supply. It is also imperative that the diver's air cylinder and breathing regulator be properly maintained. It is not uncommon for me to have my tanks visually inspected and my regulators completely overhauled twice a year.

Underwater photography often requires many dives in a single day, which may add up to several underwater hours per day. In addition, some of the most scenic reefs may be in deeper water between seventy and one hundred twenty feet. To avoid the dreaded diving disease known as the bends (too much time at depth without adequate decompression causes crippling nitrogen bubbles to form in the diver's bloodstream and tissues), the diver must be vigilant at keeping track of the depth and duration of all dives as well as the time spent on the surface between dives. Although special tables developed by the U.S. Navy and others have been available for many years to determine decompression information, in recent years, to help with decompression calculations, I've opted to use a diving computer. My choice has been the EDGE decompression meter, manufactured by Orca Industries.

Photographic Equipment

I used Nikon 35mm cameras and lenses and Kodak film exclusively to photograph the images for *California Reefs*. My workhorse system in recent years has been the Nikon F3 camera with MD4 motor drive housed in the Aquatica IIIN cast-aluminum housing, manufactured by Aqua Visions, Inc., of Montreal, Canada. I have been extremely satisfied with my Aquatica housings and find them to be rugged, reliable, very good optically, and easily operated even with diving gloves. By removing the standard viewing prism from the F3 and replacing it with a Nikon DA2 oversized sportfinder or viewfinder, I am able to have full-frame reflex viewing, even while wearing a dive mask, by peering into a special viewfinder port in the rear of the housing.

I use several wide-angle lenses in conjunction with eight-inch dome ports, which correct for focal-length loss in water and restore color saturation. My choice of Nikon wide-angle lenses for underwater use are the 16mm full-frame fisheye, 15mm rectilinear, 20mm, and 24mm. I also use a 105mm macro lens with an extension snoot and flat port (the port is the watertight "window" attached to the camera housing through which the taking lens sees into the water), which allows me to use the lens's full range of focus. Although flat ports work very well with longer-focal-length lenses, they work terribly with wide-angle lenses. As light rays travel underwater, strike a flat port from an oblique angle, and then enter a lens, refraction takes place at the water/Plexiglas/air (most camera ports for underwater still photography are made of optical-grade plastics that have excellent light-transmitting properties in water; some, however, are made of glass) interfaces. The net result is that the lens suffers a telephoto effect because of the water's magnification properties. A 35mm above-water lens actually has the apparent focal length of a 47mm lens when used underwater behind a flat port. Flat ports can also introduce problems with color because different-colored light rays refract differently when passing between mediums of unequal densities at angles other than the perpendicular. This causes color fringing and loss of color saturation and is especially noticeable with wide-angle lenses. Generally, when a wide-angle lens is used behind a flat port, the middle of the image will exhibit the least amount of distortion in focal length and color (the very center of the image may be tack sharp, actually); the edges of the image, however, where the bending of light rays is most severe, are most distorted. Dome ports minimize these two major problems by allowing light rays to strike the port at the perpendicular from all directions and thus eliminate refraction.

Although dome ports correct wide-angle lenses for underwater use, they do require some adjustments. When a dome is placed in water with air on the opposite side, the dome in fact becomes a negative diverging lens with a nonreal or virtual image that is located at a distance much closer than the apparent subject distance. A rough rule of thumb for figuring virtual image distance is that for a subject at infinity underwater (a somewhat questionable distance since a hundred feet can be a long way away underwater!), the virtual image will lie at a distance approximately twice the diameter of the dome. Therefore to focus on a subject at infinity with my eight-inch Aquatica ports, I would focus my lens at sixteen inches. As it works out, wide-angle photography with dome ports is really close-up photography. When focusing on a subject four feet away underwater with the same dome, my lens focus reading is approximately fifteen inches. These focusing adjustments are actually quite simple, especially with reflex viewing, because what you see is what you get, but with some older-style wide-angle lenses—that are not close focusing—a close-up diopter may be necessary to focus with a dome port. Longer-focal-length lenses—longer than 50mm (on a 35mm camera)—work well behind flat ports simply because the lens has a narrower field of view; light rays are entering more or less at the perpendicular, and the negative effects of refraction are negligible.

In addition to my Aquatica housings, I also use a cast-aluminum Hydro 35 housing, manufactured by Oceanic USA. I bought my Hydro 35 many years ago, before the advent of the Aquatica, and I must say this trusty housing has served me well over the years. Although it has both dome and flat ports, I use mine mostly for macro work with a flat port and have dedicated it to a 55mm f3.5 micro Nikkor with a Nikon F2 body and DA1 viewfinder, which in similar fashion to the Aquatica, affords full-frame reflex viewing.

Although I use housings for most of my work, I also own and use several Nikonos cameras. Manufactured by Nikon, Nikonos does not have reflex viewing and is sometimes called an "integral" underwater camera because it is waterproof unto itself and does not require a housing. Several models of this camera have been built over the years as it has been refined and improved (from models I through V); I still use the older Nikonos IIs and IIIs with 15mm, 28mm, and 35mm lenses and a series of macro extension tubes for the 28mm and 35mm lenses. Although several images in this book are taken with Nikonos cameras with extension tubes on a 35mm lens, I don't use them very much anymore now that I have housed reflex cameras with more versatile macro lenses. For my Nikonos cameras, I have a couple of special base plates that allow me to attach either one or two strobes as well as an underwater light meter. My choice for an underwater light meter is the Sekonic Marine Meter II, which I mount to my camera base trays with a cast-aluminum bracket manufactured by Oceanic USA.

Lighting is extremely important in underwater photography because of the selective absorption of color in seawater. As white light travels vertically down through the water column, long wavelengths of light—the reds—are filtered out first and the shortest wave lengths—the blues—are filtered out last. Generally, (and these depths vary with water clarity) the reds disappear by fifteen to twenty feet; orange is absorbed by thirty to forty feet; and by the time a diver descends to seventy feet or so the greens also disappear. Diving at eighty or ninety feet often reveals a monochromatic blue-gray world. Sometimes this monochromatic light is desirable and quite beautiful for certain types of shots, but to restore the reds, oranges, and yellows that would be seen in shallower water, some means of artificial light must be introduced.

For underwater still photography, electronic strobes are the most practical means of supplemental lighting. Even with the most powerful strobes, however, the warm colors will be quickly lost because of horizontal color absorption; at ten feet from a subject, light from a strobe must travel ten feet to the subject and then reflect back another ten feet to the camera. This total travel distance of twenty feet is enough to filter out all of the red light from the strobe; for this reason, even the best underwater strobes are not very effective beyond eight feet or so.

My workhorse strobes are a series of Oceanic 2003 strobes, used with various diffusion panels that I made myself. For some of the images in this book I also used an Oceanic 2001 model strobe, but several years ago I had it converted by the manufacturer to a model 2003, which I prefer because it has an additional low-power setting. Over the years, I've found my Oceanic strobes to be very reliable and relatively maintenance free. I also use a Graflex/Subsea Mark 150 strobe, which I love because of its even wide-angle white-beaded reflector and three-way power setting, which offers 150-, 100-, and 50-watt-second output as well as a slave setting. In addition to these powerful wide-angle strobes, I also use smaller Sonic Research SR3000 and SR2000 strobes (both sync and slave models), chiefly for fill lighting, especially when doing macro work. For the most part, my approach to underwater lighting is to strive for a qualified, naturally lit appearance in my images. Sometimes I must use two powerful wide-angle strobes attached to my housing with two long strobe arms to add fill lighting to a reef ledge, for example; this is especially important when using super-wide-angle lenses such as the 16mm full-frame fisheye. In other instances, when using a Nikonos with a 15mm lens, I may use one wide-angle strobe—perhaps my Subsea MK 150—which covers the field of view of the 15mm quite well if positioned correctly. I almost always use two strobes for my macro work; normally, I position a powerful wide-angle strobe for a key light from above, often straight down on top of my subject, just like the angle of the sun underwater. I then use one of my smaller SR3000s just off the lens axis to add fill lighting to the shadows created by the key light. I find it useful to position all my strobes with support arms and to secure them to my camera. My choice for strobe arms has been the Oceanic USA ball joint arms, which are manufactured in several different lengths.

Several of the images in *California Reefs* were taken with pieces of equipment I no longer use. One is an old Honeywell 700 Strobonar electronic flash in a special cast-aluminum housing called the Hydro Strobe II. I also had a plastic housing for this same strobe that was made by Ikelite Underwater Products. Although I retired my old Strobonar many years ago, it was my first underwater strobe, purchased when I was fourteen and used on some of my first California photo dives. I also once used a Seacor 21mm underwater lens manufactured for Nikonos cameras. Though it was a great little lens, mine simply wore out from use, and it now sits on a closet shelf in pieces.

Last but certainly not least, the film I used throughout this book—and use for all of my undersea work, for that matter—is Kodak Kodachrome 25, 64, and 200. In years past, I used Kodachrome 25 for all of my macro work, and 64 for almost everything else. In low-light situations or when shooting fast action—such as with blue sharks or sea lions—I also relied on Ektachrome 200 because I simply needed the extra film speed. In recent years, with the advent of Kodachrome 200 Professional, I have stopped using Ektachrome in favor of the new high-speed Kodachrome. In recent years I have made Kodachrome 64 Professional my standard film—I shoot everything with it including macro. When I'm faced with a low-light situation, I then use Kodachrome 200 Professional. A photographer's choice of films is really a personal matter, however, and I firmly believe that there is no one perfect film for everybody. For my needs, I find Kodachrome's fine-grain structure and accurate "normal" rendition of colors highly desirable.

Appendix II

NOTES ON THE COLOR PLATES

The following notes are intended to give more detailed information on the photographs included in *California Reefs* and the photographic techniques used in obtaining them. In addition to providing a full description of underwater housings, cameras, lenses, lighting equipment, and film, I've also included specific information on each image with regard to location, depth, and species identification. As much as possible, I've tried to include both the common and scientific names of subjects. When it was not possible from the photograph to identify positively the animal or plant as to exact species, I have named the genus only.

Over the years, I've managed to keep a detailed photo log with locations and technical information on every roll of film I've shot off the California coast. Although sometimes I've recorded photographic information several days after exposing the film, by and large it has become a ritual for me at the end of each diving day to jot down the vital statistics of the day's photographic work. This information is not only invaluable for completing a book project such as this, but is also very useful for revisiting the same reefs at a later date and for evaluating exposed film when it's returned from the lab. Unfortunately, many evenings I barely had enough energy to eat dinner and reload my cameras after a full day of diving—a day that might have also included a night dive—and my log entries at those times, out of necessity, became very streamlined.

Thus I apologize if my locations are not always as specific as they could be. The reason that some images are listed as having been taken at "Santa Catalina Island," whereas others are from "Santa Catalina Island at Stony Point," for example, is that at the time I recorded the pertinent information, my mind was willing, but my body wasn't. So I fell asleep.

FRONT COVER Giant kelp *(Macrocystis pyrifera)* detail, San Clemente Island, 40 feet. Hydro 35 housing, Nikon F2, 55mm f3.5 lens with Oceanic 2003 and Sonic Research SR2000 strobes, Kodachrome 64.

FRONT COVER INSET Blood star *(Henricia leviuscula)* on coralline algae, San Clemente Island, 75 feet. Nikonos II, 35 mm f2.5 lens with Hydro Photo close-up diopter, Oceanic 2001 strobe, Kodachrome 64.

PLATE 1. Norris' top snail *(Norrisia norrisi)*, San Clemente Island, 30 feet. Nikonos III, 35 mm f2.5 lens with 3:1 extension tube, Oceanic 2001 strobe, Kodachrome 25.

PLATE 2. Giant kelp *(Macrocystis pyrifera)* forest with garibaldi *(Hypsypops rubicundus)*, Santa Catalina Island near Cape Cortez, 40 feet. Aquatica IIIN housing, Nikon F3, 20mm f3.5 lens, Oceanic 2003 strobe, Kodachrome 200 Professional.

PLATE 3. Club anemone *(Corynactis californica)* colony, Monterey at Stillwater Cove, 50 feet. Hydro 35 housing, Nikon F2, 55mm f3.5 macro lens, Oceanic 2003 and Sonic Research strobes, Kodachrome 64 Professional.

PLATE 4. Jack mackerel *(Trachurus symmetricus)*, Santa Catalina Island at Isthmus Reef, 40 feet. Aquatica IIIN housing, Nikon F3, 105mm f2.8 macro lens, Oceanic 2003 and Sonic Research SR3000 strobes, Kodachrome 64.

PLATE 5. Reef ledge featuring red club anemones (*Corynactis californica*) and orange California hydrocoral (*Allopora californica*), Monterey at Cypress Point, 50 feet. Aquatica IIIN housing, Nikon F3, 16mm f2.8 full-frame fisheye lens, Graflex/Subsea Mark 150 strobe, Kodachrome 64 Professional.

PLATE 6. Blackeye goby (*Coryphopterus nicholsii*) on mussel shells (*Mytilus californianus*) with orange sea cucumbers (*Cucumaria miniata*), Santa Cruz Island near Pelican's Landing, 25 feet. Aquatica IIIN housing, Nikon F3, 105mm f2.8 macro lens, Oceanic 2003 and Sonic Research SR3000 strobes, Kodachrome 64 Professional.

PLATE 7. Reef ledge detail with leather star (*Dermasterias imbricata*) and orange hydrocoral (*Allopora californica*), Carmel at Inner Carmel Pinnacle, 60 feet. Aquatica IIIN housing, Nikon F3, 16mm f2.8 full-frame fisheye lens, two Oceanic 2003 strobes, Kodachrome 64 Professional.

PLATE 8. Spanish shawl nudibranch (*Flabellinopsis iodinea*) on elkhorn kelp (*Pelagophycus porra*) with encrusting bryozoans (*Membranipora* sp.), Santa Catalina Island at Stony Point, 40 feet. Hydro 35 housing, Nikon F2, 55mm f3.5 macro lens, Oceanic 2003 and Sonic Research SR3000 strobes, Kodachrome 64 Professional.

PLATE 9. Giant kelpfish (*Heterostichus rostratus*), Santa Catalina Island at Isthmus Reef, 30 feet. Aquatica IIIN housing, Nikon F3, 20mm f3.5 lens, Oceanic 2003 strobe, Kodachrome 64 Professional.

PLATE 10. Two-spotted octopus (*Octopus bimaculatus*) silhouette, Santa Rosa Island, 40 feet. Aquatica IIIN housing, Nikon F3, 20mm f3.5 lens, available light, Kodachrome 64 Professional.

PLATE 11. Yellow zooanthid anemones (*Parazoanthus lucificum*) on gorgonian (*Muricea fructicosa*), Santa Catalina Island, 30 feet. Hydro 35 housing, Nikon F2, Oceanic 2003 and Sonic Research SR2000 strobes, Kodachrome 64. When I photographed these anemones, they had completely enveloped a branch of a brown gorgonian that could eventually die as the result of their encroachment.

PLATE 12. Surfgrass (*Phyllospadix scouleri*) detail, Santa Barbara Island, 30 feet. Aquatica IIIN housing, Nikon F3, 105mm macro lens, Oceanic 2003 and Sonic Research SR3000 strobes, Kodachrome 64 Professional.

PLATE 13. Red gorgonian (*Lophogorgia chilensis*) detail, Santa Cruz Island, 40 feet. Nikonos II, 35mm f2.5 lens with 2:1 extension tube, Oceanic 2003 and Sonic Research SR3000 strobes, Kodachrome 25.

PLATE 14. California sea hare *(Aplysia californica)* skin pattern, Anacapa Island, 25 feet. Hydro 35 housing, Nikon F2, 55mm f3.5 macro lens, Oceanic 2003 and Sonic Research SR 3000 strobes, Kodachrome 64 Professional.

PLATE 15. Blacksmith *(Chromis punctipinnis)* school in giant kelp *(Macrocystis pyrifera)* forest, Santa Barbara Island at Sutil Rock, 40 feet. Aquatica IIIN housing, Nikon F3, 16mm f2.8 full-frame fisheye lens, Oceanic 2003 strobe, Kodachrome 64 Professional.

PLATE 16. Giant kelp *(Macrocystis pyrifera)* detail showing apical tip of frond, Santa Catalina Island near Cape Cortez, 50 feet. Hydro 35 housing, Nikon F2, 55mm f3.5 macro lens, Oceanic 2003 and Sonic Research SR3000 strobes, Kodachrome 64.

PLATE 17. Giant kelp *(Macrocystis pyrifera)* canopy viewed from just under ocean surface, Santa Barbara Island, 3 feet. Nikonos III, 15mm f2.8 lens, Oceanic 2003 strobe, Kodachrome 64.

PLATE 18. Giant kelp *(Macrocystis pyrifera)* haptera detail, Santa Catalina Island at Isthmus Reef, 50 feet. Hydro 35 housing, Nikon F2, 55mm f3.5 macro lens, Oceanic 2003 and Sonic Research SR3000 strobes, Kodachrome 64 Professional.

PLATE 19. Swell shark *(Cephaloscyllium ventriosum)* egg casing attached to giant kelp *(Macrocystis pyrifera)* holdfast haptera, Santa Catalina Island at Isthmus Reef, 40 feet. Aquatica IIIN housing, Nikon F3, 105mm f2.8 macro lens, Oceanic 2003 and Sonic Research SR3000 strobes, Kodachrome 64 Professional.

PLATE 20. Vertical view of giant kelp *(Macrocystis pyrifera)* forest with holdfast in foreground, Santa Barbara Island near Sutil Rock, 70 feet. Nikonos III, 15mm f2.8 lens, Oceanic 2003 strobe, Ektachrome 200.

PLATE 21. Giant kelpfish *(Gibbonsia* sp.*)* detail, Santa Catalina Island at Eagle Reef, 45 feet. Hydro 35 housing, Nikon F2, 55mm f3.5 macro lens, Oceanic 2003 and Sonic Research SR3000 strobes, Kodachrome 64.

PLATE 22. Giant kelp *(Macrocystis pyrifera)* detail showing stipe, pneumatocysts, and blades encrusted with bryozoans *(Membranipora* sp.*)*, Santa Catalina Island near Cape Cortez, 50 feet. Hydro 35 housing, Nikon F2, 55mm f3.5 macro lens, Oceanic 2003 and Sonic Research SR3000 strobes, Kodachrome 64.

PLATE 23. Anthopleura anemone *(Anthopleura* sp.*)* on giant kelp *(Macrocystis pyrifera)* holdfast haptera, Santa Barbara Island, 60 feet. Hydro 35 housing, Nikon F2, 55mm f3.5 macro lens, Oceanic 2003 and Sonic Research SR3000 strobes, Kodachrome 64 Professional.

PLATE 24. Giant kelpfish (*Heterostichus rostratus*) nestled within giant kelp (*Macrocystis pyrifera*) fronds, Santa Catalina Island at Bird Rock, 40 feet. Aquatica IIIN housing, Nikon F3, 105mm f2.8 macro lens, Oceanic 2003 and Sonic Research SR3000 strobes, Kodachrome 64 Professional.

PLATE 25. California sea lions (*Zalophus californianus*), Santa Barbara Island, 50 feet. Aquatica IIIN housing, Nikon F3, 16mm f2.8 full-frame fisheye lens, available light, Kodachrome 200 Professional.

PLATE 26. Giant kelpfish (*Heterostichus rostratus*) near holdfast of giant kelp (*Macrocystis pyrifera*), Santa Catalina Island at Isthmus Reef, 40 feet. Aquatica IIIN housing, Nikon F3, 20mm f3.5 lens, Oceanic 2003 strobe, Kodachrome 64 Professional.

PLATE 27. Norris' top snail (*Norrisia norrisi*) with calcareous coralline algae and barnacle (*Balanus* sp.) encrusting its shell, Santa Cruz Island, 50 feet. Hydro 35 housing, Nikon F2, 55mm f3.5 macro lens, Oceanic 2003 and Sonic Research SR2000 strobes, Kodachrome 64.

PLATE 28. Carinated dove snail (*Alia carinata*— formerly *Mitrella carinata*) on giant kelp (*Macrocystis pyrifera*) pneumatocyst, Santa Catalina Island, 30 feet. Nikonos II, 35mm f2.5 lens with 1:1 extension tube, Oceanic 2001 strobe, Kodachrome 25.

PLATE 29. Norris' top snail (*Norrisia norrisi*) on giant kelp (*Macrocystis pyrifera*) stipe, San Clemente Island, 50 feet. Nikonos III, 35mm f2.5 lens with Hydro Photo close-up diopter lens, Oceanic 2001 strobe, Kodachrome 25.

PLATE 30. Purple-ringed top snail *Calliostoma annulatum*) on giant kelp (*Macrocystis pyrifera*), Monterey at harbor breakwater, 30 feet. Hydro 35 housing, Nikon F2, 55mm f3.5 macro lens, Oceanic 2003 and Sonic Research SR3000 strobes, Kodachrome 64 Professional.

PLATE 31. California sea hare (*Aplysia californica*) on giant kelp (*Macrocystis pyrifera*) blade, Santa Barbara Island, 50 feet. Hydro 35 housing, Nikon F2, 55mm f3.5 lens, Oceanic 2003 and Sonic Research SR3000 strobes, Kodachrome 64 Professional.

PLATE 32. Aging giant kelp (*Macrocystis pyrifera*) blades showing eroded surface and encrusting bryozoans, Santa Catalina Island near Cape Cortez, 50 feet. Hydro 35 housing, Nikon F2, 55mm f3.5 macro lens, Oceanic 2003 and Sonic Research SR3000 strobes, Kodachrome 64.

PLATE 33. Encrusting bryozoans (*Membranipora* sp.), San Clemente Island, west end, 40 feet. Nikonos III, 35mm f2.5 lens with 1:2 macro extension tube, two Sonic Research SR3000 strobes, Kodachrome 64 Professional.

Plate 34.   Encrusting bryozoans (whitish material is *Membranipora* sp., brownish branching material is *Bugula* sp.) on aging giant kelp *(Macrocystis pyrifera)* blades, Santa Catalina Island at Rock Quarry, 40 feet. Hydro 35 housing, Nikon F2, 55mm f3.5 macro lens, Oceanic 2003 and Sonic Research SR3000 strobes, Kodachrome 64.

Plate 35.   Blood star *(Henricia leviuscula)* near giant kelp *(Macrocystis pyrifera)* holdfast, San Clemente Island at Castle Rock, 40 feet. Hydro 35 housing, Nikon F2, 55mm f3.5 macro lens, Oceanic 2003 and Sonic Research SR3000 strobes, Kodachrome 64.

Plate 36.   California spiny lobster *(Panulirus interruptus)* on giant kelp *(Macrocystis pyrifera)* stalk, San Nicolas Island, 45 feet. Hydro 35 housing, Nikon F2, 55mm f3.5 macro lens, Oceanic 2003 and Sonic Research SR3000 strobes, Kodachrome 64 Professional.

Plate 37.   Garibaldi *(Hypsypops rubicundus)* in giant kelp *(Macrocystis pyrifera)* forest, Santa Catalina Island at Emerald Bay, 40 feet. Aquatica IIIN housing, Nikon F3, 16mm f2.8 full-frame fisheye lens, Oceanic 2003 strobe, Kodachrome 64 Professional.

Plate 38.   California sea lion *(Zalophus californianus)* in giant kelp *(Macrocystis pyrifera)* forest, Santa Barbara Island, 30 feet. Nikonos III, 15mm f2.8 lens, available light, Ektachrome 200.

Plate 39.   California sea otter *(Enhydra lutris)*, Monterey at Lovers' Cove, 3 feet. Aquatica IIIN housing, Nikon F3, 20mm f3.5 lens, Oceanic 2003 strobe, Ektachrome 200.

Plate 40.   Harbor seal *(Phoca vitulina)* in giant kelp *(Macrocystis pyrifera)* forest, Monterey off Cannery Row, 25 feet. Aquatica IIIN housing, Nikon F3, 20mm f3.5 lens, Oceanic 2003 strobe, Ektachrome 200.

Plate 41.   Lion nudibranch *(Melibe leonina)* on giant kelp *(Macrocystis pyrifera)* blade, Monterey near harbor breakwater, 20 feet. Hydro 35 housing, Nikon F2, 55mm f3.5 macro lens, Oceanic 2003 and Sonic Research SR3000 strobes, Kodachrome 64 Professional.

Plate 42.   Black-speckled sea lemon nudibranch *(Anisodoris nobilis)* egg ribbon on giant kelp *(Macrocystis pyrifera)* blade, Santa Rosa Island, 40 feet. Hydro 35 housing, Nikon F2, 55mm f3.5 macro lens, Oceanic 2003 and Sonic Research SR 3000 strobes, Kodachrome 64.

Plate 43.   Northern kelp crab *(Pugettia producta)* on giant kelp *(Macrocystis pyrifera)* blade, Monterey near harbor breakwater, 20 feet. Hydro 35 housing, Nikon F2, 55mm f3.5 macro lens, Oceanic 2003 and Sonic Research SR3000 strobes, Kodachrome 64 Professional.

PLATE 44. Giant kelp (*Macrocystis pyrifera*) blade detail with small developing bryozoan (*Membranipora* sp.) masses, Santa Barbara Island, 20 feet. Nikonos II, 35mm f2.5 lens with 1:1 macro extension tube, Oceanic 2003 and Sonic Research SR2000 strobes, Kodachrome 25.

PLATE 45. Reef ledge detail featuring purple hydrocoral (*Allopora californica*), orange bat star (*Patiria miniata*), giant spined star (*Pisaster giganteus*), and blood star (*Henricia leviuscula*), Carmel off Cypress Point, 50 feet. Nikonos III, 15mm f2.8 lens, Graflex/ Subsea Mark 150 strobe, Kodachrome 200 Professional.

PLATE 46. Purple sea urchins (*Strongylocentrotus purpuratus*) with rock scallop (*Hinnites giganteus*) shell, Santa Cruz Island near Cavern Point, 40 feet. Hydro 35 housing, Nikon F2, 55mm f3.5 macro lens, Oceanic 2003 and Sonic Research SR3000 strobes, Kodachrome 64 Professional.

PLATE 47. Reef ledge with orange hydrocoral (*Allopora californica*), Carmel off Cypress Point, 50 feet. Nikonos III, 15mm f2.8 lens, Graflex/Subsea Mark 150 strobe, Kodachrome 200 Professional.

PLATE 48. Giant spined star (*Pisaster giganteus*) with purple hydrocoral (*Allopora californica*), Santa Barbara Island, 80 feet. Hydro 35 housing, Nikon F2, 55mm f3.5 macro lens, Oceanic 2003 and Sonic Research SR3000 strobes, Kodachrome 64 Professional.

PLATE 49. Leafy hornmouth snail (*Ceratostoma foliatum*), Santa Catalina Island at Cortez Rock, 40 feet. Aquatica IIIN Housing, Nikon F3, 105mm f2.8 macro lens, Oceanic 2003 and Sonic Research SR3000 strobes, Kodachrome 64 Professional.

PLATE 50. Sea urchin (*Strongylocentrotus* sp.) test, Santa Catalina Island, 30 feet. Hydro 35 housing, Nikon F2, 55mm f3.5 macro lens, Oceanic 2003 and Sonic Research SR2000 strobes, Kodachrome 64.

PLATE 51. Spanish shawl nudibranch (*Flabellinopsis iodinea*), Santa Barbara at Stern's Wharf, 15 feet. Nikonos II, 35mm f2.5 lens with 1:1 macro extension tube, Honeywell 700 Strobonar in Hydro Strobe II housing, Kodachrome 25.

PLATE 52. Plume worms (*Spirobranchus spinosus*), Santa Catalina Island near Ribbon Rock, 50 feet. Hydro 35 housing, Nikon F2, 55mm f3.5 macro lens, Oceanic 2003 and Sonic Research SR3000 strobes, Kodachrome 64 Professional.

PLATE 53. Rainbow sea star (*Orthasterias koehleri*) skin pattern detail, Santa Cruz Island, 25 feet. Aquatica IIIN housing, Nikon F3, 105mm f2.8 macro lens, Oceanic 2003 and Sonic Research SR3000 strobes, Kodachrome 64 Professional.

PLATE 54. Giant spined star (*Pisaster giganteus*) skin pattern detail, Santa Cruz Island, 25 feet. Aquatica IIIN housing, Nikon F3, 105mm f2.8 macro lens, Oceanic 2003 and Sonic Research SR3000 strobes, Kodachrome 64 Professional.

PLATE 55. Surfgrass (*Phyllospadix scouleri*) photographed at ¼ second shutter speed with wave surge, Cortez Bank, 60 feet. Nikonos III, 15mm f2.8 lens, Oceanic 2003 strobe, Kodachrome 64 Professional.

PLATE 56. Abalone (*Haliotis* sp.) shell with coralline algae and plume worm (*Spirobranchus* sp.), Santa Catalina Island near Ribbon Rock, 60 feet. Hydro 35 housing, Nikon F2, 55mm f3.5 macro lens, Oceanic 2003 and Sonic Research SR2000 strobes, Kodachrome 64.

PLATE 57. Rock scallop (*Hinnites giganteus*) shell with coralline algae and orange cup corals (*Balanophyllia elegans*), Santa Catalina Island, 30 feet. Hydro 35 housing, Nikon F2, 55mm f3.5 macro lens, Oceanic 2003 and Sonic Research SR2000 strobes, Kodachrome 64.

PLATE 58. Garibaldi (*Hypsypops rubicundus*), Santa Catalina Island at Stony Point, 40 feet. Hydro 35 housing, Nikon F2, 55mm f3.5 macro lens, Oceanic 2003 strobe, Kodachrome 64.

PLATE 59. Blue-banded goby (*Lythrypnus dalli*) with plume worm (*Spyrobranchus* sp.), Corynactis anemones (*Corynactis californica*), and bryozoans (*Bugula* sp.) in foreground, Santa Catalina at Isthmus Reef, 40 feet. Aquatica IIIN housing, Nikon F3, 105mm f2.8 macro lens, Oceanic 2003 and Sonic Research SR3000 strobes, Kodachrome 64 Professional.

PLATE 60. Island kelpfish (*Alloclinus holderi*), Santa Catalina Island at Bird Rock, 40 feet. Aquatica IIIN housing, Nikon F3, 105mm f2.8 macro lens, Oceanic 2003 and Sonic Research SR3000 strobes, Kodachrome 64 Professional.

PLATE 61. Garibaldis (*Hypsypops rubicundus*), Santa Barbara Island, 75 feet. Nikonos III, 15mm f2.8 lens, Oceanic 2003 strobe, Kodachrome 64.

PLATE 62. Hermit crab (*Paguristes* sp.) inside wavy top snail (*Astraea undosa*) shell, Santa Catalina Island at Bird Rock, 40 feet. Aquatica IIIN housing, Nikon F3, 105mm f2.8 macro lens, Oceanic 2003 and Sonic Research SR3000 strobes, Kodachrome 64 Professional.

PLATE 63. California moray eel (*Gymnothorax mordax*), San Clemente Island, 90 feet. Hydro 35 housing, Nikon F2, Oceanic 2003 and Sonic Research SR2000 strobes, Kodachrome 64.

PLATE 64. Octopus (*Octopus* sp.) under reef ledge, Santa Catalina Island, 50 feet. Hydro 35 housing, Nikon F2, 55mm f3.5 macro lens, Oceanic 2003 and Sonic Research SR2000 strobes, Kodachrome 64.

PLATE 65. California spiny lobster (*Panulirus interruptus*), San Clemente Island, 80 feet. Hydro 35 housing, Nikon F2, 55mm f3.5 macro lens, Oceanic 2003 and Sonic Research SR2000 strobes, Kodachrome 64.

PLATE 66. Island kelpfish (*Alloclinus holderi*), Santa Catalina Island at Hen Rock, 40 feet. Nikonos II, 35mm f2.5 lens with 1:1 macro extension tube, Oceanic 2003 and Sonic Research SR2000 strobes, Kodachrome 64.

PLATE 67. White-spotted rose anemone (*Tealia lofotensis*), Monterey off Mono Lobo Point, 80 feet. Hydro 35 housing, Nikon F2, 55mm f3.5 macro lens, Oceanic 2003 and Sonic Research SR3000 strobes, Kodachrome 64 Professional.

PLATE 68. Giant green anemone (*Anthopleura xanthogrammica*), San Nicolas Island, 30 feet. Hydro 35 housing, Nikon F2, 55mm f3.5 macro lens, Oceanic 2003 and Sonic Research SR3000 strobes, Kodachrome 64 Professional.

PLATE 69. Orange cup coral (*Balanophyllia elegans*), San Clemente Island, 30 feet. Nikonos II, 35mm f2.5 lens with 1:1 macro extension tube, Oceanic 2003 and Sonic Research SR2000 strobes, Kodachrome 25.

PLATE 70. Club anemone (*Corynactis californica*), Santa Barbara at Stern's Wharf, 20 feet. Nikonos II, 35mm f2.5 lens with 1:1 macro extension tube, Honeywell 700 Strobonar with Ikelite underwater housing, Kodachrome 25.

PLATE 71. Spanish shawl nudibranch (*Flabellinopsis iodinea*), Anacapa Island, 25 feet. Nikonos II, 35mm f2.5 lens with 1:2 macro extension tube, Honeywell 700 Strobonar with Ikelite underwater housing, Kodachrome 25.

PLATE 72. Horned nudibranch (*Hermissenda crassicornis*) on bryozoans (*Bugula* sp.), San Nicolas Island, 60 feet. Hydro 35 housing, Nikon F2, 55mm f3.5 macro lens, Oceanic 2003 and 2001 strobes, Kodachrome 64.

PLATE 73. Rose anemone (*Tealia piscivora*), Monterey off Mono Lobo Point, 80 feet. Aquatica IIIN housing, Nikon F3, 16mm f2.8 full-frame fisheye lens, Graflex/Subsea Mark 150 strobe, Kodachrome 200 Professional.

PLATE 74. Jack mackerel (*Trachurus symmetricus*) school, Santa Catalina Island at Hen Rock, 30 feet. Nikonos III, 15mm f2.8 lens, available light, Kodachrome 64 Professional.

PLATE 75. Pacific angel shark (*Squatina californica*) eye detail, Santa Cruz Island west of Cavern Point, 30 feet. Hydro 35 housing, Nikon F2, 55mm f3.5 macro lens, Oceanic 2003 and Sonic Research SR3000 strobes, Kodachrome 64 Professional.

PLATE 76. Channeled nassa (*Nassarius nassa*), Monterey near harbor breakwater, 10 feet. Aquatica IIIN housing, Nikon F3, 105mm f2.8 macro lens, Oceanic 2003 and Sonic Research SR3000 strobes, Kodachrome 64 Professional.

Plate 77. Wavy turban snail *(Astraea undosa)* encrusted with coralline algae, Santa Catalina Island near Isthmus Reef, 50 feet. Hydro 35 housing, Nikon F2, 55mm f3.5 macro lens, Oceanic 2003 and Sonic Research and SR 3000 strobes, Kodachrome 64 Professional.

Plate 78. Bat stars *(Patiria miniata)*, Monterey at harbor breakwater, 25 feet. Hydro 35 housing, Nikon F2, 55mm f3.5 macro lens, Oceanic 2003 and Sonic Research SR2000 strobes, Kodachrome 64 Professional.

Plate 79. Bat stars *(Patiria miniata)* with nudibranch egg ribbon, Monterey near harbor breakwater, 25 feet. Hydro 35 housing, Nikon F2, 55mm f3.5 macro lens, Oceanic 2003 and Sonic Research SR3000 strobes, Kodachrome 64 Professional.

Plate 80. Bat star *(Patiria miniata)* skin pattern detail, Monterey at Lovers' Cove, 20 feet. Hydro 35 housing, Nikon F2, 55mm f3.5 macro lens with PK 3 extension ring, Oceanic 2003 and Sonic Research SR3000 strobes, Kodachrome 64 Professional.

Plate 81. Blackeye goby *(Coryphopterus nicholsii)* on orange bat star *(Patiria miniata)*, Monterey at harbor breakwater, 40 feet. Aquatica IIIN housing, Nikon F3, 105mm f2.8 macro lens, Oceanic 2003 and Sonic Research SR3000 strobes, Kodachrome 64 Professional.

Plate 82. Twenty-foot-long basking shark *(Cetorhinus maximus)*, feeding just beneath ocean surface, Santa Barbara Channel near Carpenteria, 5 feet. Nikonos II, Seacor 21mm f3.5 lens, available light, Ektachrome 200.

Plate 83. Pacific angel shark *(Squatina californica)*, Santa Catalina Island near Hen Rock, 50 feet. Aquatica IIIN housing, Nikon F3, 15mm f3.5 rectilinear lens, Graflex/Subsea Mark 150 strobe, Kodachrome 64 Professional.

Plate 84. Blue shark *(Prionace glauca)*, near Santa Cruz Island in the Anacapa Passage, 20 feet. Nikonos II, Seacor 21mm f3.5 lens, available light, Ektachrome 200.

Plate 85. Sand dollar *(Dendraster excentricus)*, Monterey near harbor breakwater, 15 feet. Hydro 35 housing, Nikon F2, 55mm f3.5 macro lens, Oceanic 2003 and Sonic Research SR3000 strobes, Kodachrome 64 Professional.

Plate 86. Bat star *(Patiria miniata)* with tube anemone *(Pachycerianthus fimbriatus)*, Monterey near harbor breakwater, 35 feet. Hydro 35 housing, Nikon F2, 55mm f3.5 macro lens, Oceanic 2003 and Sonic Research SR3000 strobes, Kodachrome 64 Professional.

Plate 87. California halibut *(Paralichthys californicus)*, Monterey off Cannery Row, 25 feet. Aquatica IIIN housing, Nikon F3, 105mm f2.8 macro lens, Oceanic 2003 and Sonic Research SR3000 strobes, Kodachrome 64 Professional.

PLATE 88.   Rock crab *(Cancer antennarius)* shell abandoned on bottom after molting, Monterey at Point Lobos, Whalers' Cove, 25 feet. Hydro 35 housing, Nikon F2, 55mm f3.5 macro lens, Oceanic 2003 and Sonic Research SR2000 strobes, Kodachrome 64.

PLATE 89.   Pelagic red crab *(Pleuroncodes planipes)*, Santa Catalina Island near Cape Cortez, 30 feet. Hydro 35 housing, Nikon F2, 55mm f3.5 macro lens, Oceanic 2003 and Sonic Research SR3000 strobes, Kodachrome 64.

PLATE 90.   Pelagic red crab *(Pleuroncodes planipes)* silhouette, Santa Catalina Island near Cape Cortez, 40 feet. Hydro 35 housing, Nikon F2, 55mm f3.5 macro lens, Oceanic 2003 and SR3000 strobes, Kodachrome 64.

PLATE 91.   California sea lions *(Zalophus californianus)*, motor-drive sequence taken at Santa Barbara Island, 50 feet. Aquatica IIIN housing, Nikon F3, 16mm f2.8 full-frame fisheye lens, available light, Kodachrome 200 Professional.

PLATE 92.   California sea lions *(Zalophus californianus)*, Santa Barbara Island, 15 feet. Aquatica IIIN housing, Nikon F3, 16mm f2.8 full-frame fisheye lens, available light, Kodachrome 200 Professional.

PLATE 93.   Tube anemone *(Pachycerianthus fimbriatus)*, Monterey at harbor breakwater, 35 feet. Hydro 35 housing, Nikon F2, 55mm f3.5 macro lens, Oceanic 2003 and Sonic Research SR3000 strobes, Kodachrome 64 Professional.

PLATE 94.   Spiny sand star *(Astropecten armatus)*, Santa Rosa Island, 40 feet. Hydro 35 housing, Nikon F2, 55mm f3.5 macro lens, Oceanic 2003 and Sonic Research SR2000 strobes, Kodachrome 64.

PLATE 95.   Blacksmith *(Chromis punctipinnis)*, Santa Catalina Island near Hen Rock, 40 feet. Aquatica IIIN housing Nikon F3, 105mm f2.8 macro lens, Oceanic 2003 and Sonic Research SR3000 strobes, Kodachrome 64 Professional.

BACK COVER   Red gorgonian *(Lophogorgia chilensis)* with light bulb tunicates *(Clavelina huntsmani)*, Santa Catalina Island at entrance to Blue Caverns, 40 feet. Hydro 35 housing, Nikon F2, 55mm f3.5 macro lens, Oceanic 2003 and Sonic Research SR2000 strobes, Kodachrome 64.